NOTES FROM
MY TRAVELS

NOTES FROM MY TRAVELS

Visits with Refugees in Africa, Cambodia, Pakistan, and Ecuador

Angelina Jolie

POCKET BOOKS

New York   London   Toronto   Sydney

All of the author's proceeds from this book are being donated to
the United Nations High Commissioner for Refugees.

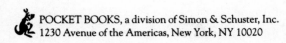 POCKET BOOKS, a division of Simon & Schuster, Inc.
1230 Avenue of the Americas, New York, NY 10020

The opinions expressed are not necessarily those of UNHCR. The designations and
maps used do not imply the expression of any opinion or recognition on the part of
UNHCR concerning the legal status of territory or of its authorities.

All maps by UNHCR (geographic data from Global Insight copyright Europa
Technologies Ltd.)

ISBN: 0-7434-7023-0

First Pocket Books trade paperback edition October 2003

10   9   8

POCKET and colophon are registered trademarks of
Simon & Schuster, Inc.

Manufactured in the United States of America

For information regarding special discounts for bulk purchases,
please contact Simon & Schuster Special Sales at 1-800-456-6798 or
business@simonandschuster.com.

Dedication

The ratio of staff members to people of concern to UNHCR: 1 staff member per 3,582 refugees. This book is dedicated to them: to their hard work and most of all their dedication and deep respect for their fellow man.

I also dedicate this book to the men, women, and children who are now or have once been refugees: to those who have survived against remarkable odds and to those who did not, those who died fighting for their freedom.

These people have taught me my greatest life lessons and for that I am forever grateful.

Contents

Foreword by the United Nations
High Commissioner for Refugees   ix

Introduction   xi

Mission to Africa   1

Mission to Cambodia   77

Mission to Pakistan   133

Mission to Ecuador   193

Afterword   237

Maps   239

Foreword by the United Nations High Commissioner for Refugees

The Office of the United Nations High Commissioner for Refugees (UNHCR) was established in 1951 to care for those forced to flee their homes because of persecution or war. Over the past five decades, UNHCR has helped an estimated 50 million men, women, and children to find safety and to restart their lives.

Our challenges are immense, and they could not be met without the dedicated support of concerned individuals around the world. One such champion of the refugee cause is Angelina Jolie.

On 27 August 2001, I named Angelina Jolie as a Goodwill Ambassador for UNHCR. Some time before this, she had shown a profound interest in refugee issues, and had visited refugee camps in places like Sierra Leone, Cambodia, and Pakistan.

In 2002 and 2003, Angelina visited refugees in Namibia, Thailand, Ecuador, Tanzania, Sri Lanka, Kosovo, and Ingushetia, and worked closely with UNHCR field staff. Her impressions are movingly recounted in these vivid personal journals. She will be making more field visits in the years ahead.

Since her appointment as a Goodwill Ambassador, Angelina has more than fulfilled my expectations. She has proven to be a close partner and a genuine colleague in our efforts to find solutions for the world's refugees. Above all, she has helped to make the tragedy of refugees real to everyone who will listen. Angelina's interest in helping refugees, her personal generosity, and her truly compassionate spirit are an inspiration to us all.

RUUD LUBBERS
U.N. High Commissioner for Refugees

Introduction

I was asked to write an introduction to my journals, to explain how my journals came to be, why my life took this direction, and why I decided to start it.

As I try to find the answers, I am sure of one thing: I am forever changed. I am so grateful I took this path in my life, thankful that I met these amazing people and had this incredible experience.

I honestly believe that if we were all aware, we would all be compelled to act.

So the question is not how or why I would do this with my life. The question is, how could I not?

Many nights I sat awake reading stories and statistics about national and international tragedies.

I read about UNHCR:

- More than twenty million refugees exist today.

- One-sixth of the world's population lives on less than one dollar a day.

- 1.1 billion people lack access to safe drinking water.

- One-third of the world has no electricity.

- More than 100 million children are out of school.

- One in six children in Africa dies before the age of five.

I read about different organizations that do humanitarian work. I had been reading about Sierra Leone when I was in England. When I got back to the States it was difficult to follow the stories, so I called USA for UNHCR and asked if they could help me understand the situation there and similar situations elsewhere in the world. Three weeks later I was in Sierra Leone.

I don't know how this will be as a book, how readers will find it. I am not a writer. These are just my journals. They are just a glimpse into a world that I am just beginning to understand, a world I could never really explain in words.

Mission to Africa

From February 22 through March 9, 2001, I undertook a mission to learn about and assist refugees under the care of the United Nations High Commissioner for Refugees (UNHCR) in Sierra Leone and Tanzania.

Tuesday, February 20

I am on a plane to Africa. I will have a two-hour layover in the Paris airport, and then on to Abidjan in Côte d'Ivoire (Ivory Coast).

This is the beginning of my trip and this journal. I do not know who I am writing to—myself, I guess, or to everyone, whoever you are. I am not writing for the person who may read these pages but for the people I will be writing about.

I honestly want to help. I don't believe I am different from other people. I think we all want justice and equality. We all want a chance for a life with meaning. All of us would like to believe that if we were in a bad situation someone would help us.

I don't know what I will accomplish on this trip. All I do know is that while I was learning more and more every day about the world and about other countries as well as my own, I realized how much I didn't know.

I have done a lot of research and talked with many people in Washington, D.C., at the United Nations High Commissioner for Refugees (UNHCR). I have read as much as I could. I discovered statistics that shocked me and stories that broke my heart. I also read many things that made me sick. I have had nightmares—not many, but they scared me.

I don't understand why some things are talked about and others are not.

I don't know why I think I can make any kind of difference. All I know is that I want to.

I wasn't sure I should go. I'm still not sure, but—and I know this may sound false to some—I thought of the people who have no choice.

It seems crazy to some of my friends that I want to leave the warmth and safety of my home. They asked, "Why can't you just help from here? Why do you have to see it?" I didn't know how to answer them. And I'm not sure if I'm being crazy or stupid.

My dad attempted to cancel my trip. He called USA for UNHCR, but since I am an adult, he couldn't stop me. I was angry with him, but I told him that I know he loves me and that as my father he was trying to protect me from harm. We embraced and smiled at one another.

My mom looked at me like I was her little girl. She smiled at me through her teary eyes. She is worried. As she hugged me good-bye, she gave me a specific message from my brother, Jamie. "Tell Angie I love her, and to remember that if she is ever scared, sad, or angry—look up at the night sky, find the second star on the right, and follow it straight on till morning." That's from *Peter Pan*, one of our favorite stories.

I am thinking about those people I have been reading so much about and how they are separated from the families they love. They have no home. They are watching the people they love die. They are dying themselves. And they have no choice.

I don't know what it will be like where I am going, but I am looking forward to meeting these people.

My first stop is Paris for a few hours and then to Africa.

Wednesday, February 21

On the plane from Paris an African man wearing a nice blue suit and a warm smile asked me if I was a journalist. I said, "No, just an American who wants to learn about Africa." He said, "Good!"

He seemed to be an important man surrounded by others in suits who greeted him as if to pay respect. As he got off the plane with the group he was traveling with, a few military men—one in front and one in back—led them out and a camera caught him as he greeted a man who must have represented another important group.

I write all this because when he asked me on the plane if I was traveling to other parts of Africa, I told him, "Sierra Leone," and he said, "I am scared of that place."

After we landed in Côte d'Ivoire, I was met at the plane by a very sweet man from UNHCR. His name is Herve. He spoke French and very little English. I speak very little French. But I realized quickly that smiles and gestures are all you really need sometimes. We stood next to each other in silence, since my bags were the last off the plane.

Everyone's bags are opened and checked.

I saw more military people than civilians.

I then met another man from UNHCR.

We talked in the car about how Sierra Leone is going through a civil war.

It is not unlike the Americans before they became what they are today. When you think about that you realize how important it is to help and support them as they determine the future of fifty-two countries on this big, powerful continent.

If we consider the people of Africa our allies and help them to build, it will only help us.

I have discovered that the United States has helped a great deal and that should not go unnoticed. But compared with so many other countries we give less (per capita). With what we have compared with others' ability to give, we give less.

Politics aside, on a human level we should all be reminded of what is important and how we are truly equal.

We should help in the beginning when people are trying and forming, not when it is too late.

During the Cold War, Africa was split. They had gained independence in the '60s, but when the Cold War was over, Africa needed help to strengthen its democracies.

It needed help in order to support those people who stood for the same freedoms we all believe in.

There was a video I saw on Sierra Leone.

They had a march for democracy a few years ago. I can't remember what year, but it was before the worst of the fighting had started.

If only we had offered our help back then, perhaps it would not be this way now.

We can't forget that our founding fathers were refugees.

And then the Native Americans became refugees.

The man who welcomed me spoke about his time in America. We both expressed an awareness of how little is told to the American people and how sheltered they can be. But to their credit, when they do see what is happening around the world (from a special on CNN to occasional stories in the newspapers), most Americans do want to help, and they are very generous.

He told me he had been to Kansas City, Missouri, for one Christmas. He also shared other stories of experiences he had in America. I thought about how he had taken the time to travel to the United States, because he "wanted to understand America a little better."

Very few of us have been to Mali (a country in Africa where he was born).

And that could be why he was so welcoming. He wanted to share his country with me.

I checked in to my room in Abidjan on the Ivory Coast. This hotel must have been beautiful once, and it is better than I had expected my accommodations to be. I feel wrong staying in this place, even though it's only for a few nights. I am here in Abidjan to have meetings with UNHCR. On Saturday I will leave for Freetown in Sierra Leone to be with the refugees.

I have to admit I do appreciate the proper shower and sleep. I know to enjoy it tonight and I am grateful.

Thursday, February 22

I am sitting in a chair in a UNHCR office here in Abidjan. I am having a long morning.

I have come to understand many things, and yet there is so much I don't understand. Most of all I realized how little awareness I had of these people.

I am sitting under a sign—a poster for UNHCR. It reads

IT DOESN'T TAKE MUCH TO BECOME A REFUGEE. YOUR RACE OR BELIEF CAN BE ENOUGH.

I was allowed to sit in on an interview with "asylum seekers."

These "asylum seekers" are here to apply for a chance to live in the borders of a country that is different from their own place of origin.

UNHCR will listen to their stories and sometimes check on the information. They will help them if they can. They have to try to determine if they are eligible to be labeled a refugee, and therefore, seek asylum.

They must prove their need for protection and support; that is, for whatever protection and support is available, and in many countries that is not much at all.

The young couple interviewed today lost contact with their two children. The husband was thirty. The wife was twenty-five (my age).

They seemed much older. Their bodies so weary, their eyes so sad, desperate. They both spoke French and a little English and were very intelligent.

They made a kind of attempt to make me feel comfortable.

When they were introduced to me, it was explained that I was an American here in Africa to try to understand and to learn in order to help express situations like theirs to my country.

I was glad I felt they understood another person was trying to help, but after hearing their story, I felt helpless and yet full of purpose at the same time.

These people are strong, smart people. Given the opportunity, and considering all the resources that are now tearing the country apart, they could be a very strong, rich country.

It may seem like groups such as UNHCR and others are not successful at times because of all that is still going on. But in learning the history of the refugee situation and understanding all the work that has been done to help them, I realized that all of these dedicated workers have been very generous with their help.

We should all be very grateful.

I believe without their intervention, the refugees would have no hope at all. Most of these groups of people would be dead and forgotten.

Everything would be in rebel hands and under the control of dictators.

We must continue to give support to help the countries in Africa that welcome the refugees and give them a home.

Our country and other countries will continue to have refugees crossing our borders unless we help strengthen the countries from which they come.

Friday, February 23

The next day I was brought into another office room where I met Ioli, who sat me down to teach me more things. She had a wonderful energy and passion and a great laugh.

I learned about new computer technologies that help count, identify, and give ID cards to refugees.

It was encouraging to hear of the different donations of equipment that have been made and the new ideas that will help.

Microsoft donated one hundred ID card machines during the crisis in Kosovo. Still, more technicians are always needed to operate them. It is amazing how many things must be thought of. They are now in the process of raising funds for a training program.

You realize being here how important these ID cards are. They are not only for protecting the refugees and proving their safe asylum. Their most important benefit is that when refugees come to register, the cards give them an individual identity.

You can imagine what it might feel like to not be able to prove who you are—no proof of your name or country or family or age.

Children with no ID can be forced into the army or into performing dangerous labor. They can be taken or withheld from school. Every child has a right to safety and education.

At lunchtime, I went to a small market to buy some local crafts.

While standing in one place too long my ankles began to itch. They were being bitten by bugs so small I couldn't even see them.

In some areas the smell was rancid. I felt sick.

The strength of survival here is amazing to me. They don't complain. They don't even beg.

Contrary to our image of this country, its people are civilized, strong, proud, stunning people. Any aggressive feeling is pure survival. There is no time for casual or lazy behavior.

As I wrote that, I realized I am writing as if I am studying people in a zoo.

I feel stupid and arrogant to think I know anything about these people and their struggles.

But I am simply making observations of the people here in Côte d'Ivoire. This is the first and only place I have been to in Africa. I haven't even seen the refugee camps yet.

There are so many school children. The boys are in beige. They are wearing short-sleeve shirts and pants. The girls are wearing white blouses and blue skirts.

In the markets there is so much gold and ivory for sale—even diamonds. Everything is piled on tables in small stacks. The floors are all of dirt.

A woman from UNHCR named Demu offered to show me around.

I met her daughter and friends. They are all fourteen years old and attend an international school. They spoke many languages. They have lived all over the world. They are all funny and each of them is a unique individual.

They dream of their futures. They all seem so much older than the teenagers in the United States.

They are all very politically aware. One girl asked me what I thought of our new American president, George W. Bush.

They also seem to know a lot about film. I hope they are seeing the good ones as well as the cool and silly ones. But here it seems just as important to laugh.

Saturday, February 24

We are waiting for our plane to Sierra Leone to fuel and for all of our passports to be checked. Ioli is with me. Although we are getting off in different places, I'm happy to start the trip with someone familiar.

They just weighed my luggage and myself . . . eight kilos . . . four kilos . . . and I weigh fifty-five kilos (whatever that means, I don't know). A man in broken sandals pulled out a plastic scale, one you would stand on in your bathroom at home. It had two pink bunnies on it, very faded. Our luggage was spilling over it as we weighed each piece. I can't imagine how they get it accurate.

I am surrounded by so many nationalities. I see a beautiful African woman in semitraditional dress.

The plane is ready, but just before we take off, we are warned to use the bathroom. It will be hours before we are near one. Ioli and I go. Everyone else waits in the hot sun. No one boards. Then I realize why: ladies first.

"Bon voyage" and "Good luck," they all say.

I am sitting in the plane now. I picked a seat with no air vent.

We have not yet taken off, but I am already sweating. I lick it off my top lip.

Everyone is smiling at each other, exchanging kind words and curiosities about what they are each doing.

They noticed the tattoo on my arm.

I was told the authorities have recently had the job of clearing out rebels who are pretending to be refugees. These rebels try to get a part of whatever small support is being handed out.

A woman said she saw many men being held (detained) for days having to prove their identity.

She asked why they were considered suspect.

"Because they have tattoos on their arms!" (It's a common tribal practice in Guinea and Sierra Leone.)

We laughed about the possibility that I could be considered a rebel by authorities.

Still, it makes you think that the symbols we wear do express ourselves. Symbols to some cause fear or are looked down upon.

I think of the choices I have made—the markings I have—the jewelry I wear:

- my brother's initial
- a quote about freedom by my favorite American writer . . .

We just landed to pick up one more person. Now there are seven of us.

It got cooler in the air. It is a beautiful day. Most of us got out and stretched for a few minutes.

When I was picked up by the bus to be taken to the plane, there were two people on board who I had not yet met—a man in front and a woman sitting near me. They both seemed not to like me, or so I assumed by their distance. We did not introduce ourselves. I was intimidated by the man. I wondered if I was going to be working with him. Later on the plane I was ashamed to realize I had judged them. I should feel lucky to be in their company.

After a while the man turned to me and explained he was held captive by the rebels in Monrovia, Liberia, for six days. They had trouble up to the last minute getting him out. He mentioned hours delayed in this airport.

When he and his wife and I finally spoke, I found them warm and kind. Their silence and the distance I felt was their feeling of horror. We landed on the same ground where he had been held captive.

Most people in this country have been through things I could never imagine.

As I stepped outside, I was told this area has no real hope. Almost everything here was burned down or shelled.

When rebels leave on foot, sometimes they take hostages simply to help them carry stolen goods back home.

From the sky everything was so beautiful—the land, the lakes, the forest—all as far as I could see.

Army helicopters are the only aircraft in this airport.

Finally we landed in Freetown, Sierra Leone. As we drove through the streets we spoke of what has been happening here. Revolutionary United Front (RUF) called it "Project No Living Thing."

I notice hundreds of people walking through the streets holding hands—survivors!

Painted on cars is GOD IS GREAT and LOVE FOR EVERYONE— HATE NO MORE.

You would think these would be the last people on earth to believe that, and yet you realize they have a deeper understanding because of all they went through.

Strange custom: On the last Saturday of every month everyone must stay home and clean their environment until 10 A.M. If you leave before then you must have a pass explaining why you have been given permission.

Saturday Night
UNHCR Guest House

Broken glass is stuck into the top of the cement walls that surround the house.

As our truck pulls up, a guard opens the wooden gate.

A small, off-white building with chipped paint and a few old cars stands beyond the gate.

I am greeted with smiles by most, stares by a few.

I am in room number 1. That's what the piece of paper stuck to my door says. I think they gave me the best they have.

I could hardly get water out of the shower. The room would be considered poor and run-down by the people from the world I live in, but certainly not by the people here. They would consider it a palace.

I am very grateful.

Dinner was at eight. Two members of the UNHCR field staff and I sat and talked about war, life, survival. They told me many things. I wish I could write every single thing down.

The television downstairs has one channel. If they are lucky, it will get CNN. It didn't tonight.

Time is different here. There is so much focus on survival. You simply live and enjoy the day and the people around you as much as you can.

People share.

I mention that this place is lacking in things not because I miss them but because I see the way the people who work here live.

Most of them are not making exceptions for themselves—some may be. I realize there are a few people in every group who are not good people. A few nongovernmental organization (NGO) and U.N. workers seem to be in a strange competition.

They help each other, and yet sometimes criticize each other—trying to hurt.

But I do believe that even the critical ones have to be a certain kind of good person. You can't be a bad person if this is what you choose to do with your life.

Sunday, February 25

I had a strange dream—not entirely bad, but bad enough to call it a nightmare.

I was being held at a checkpoint as I stood on a sidewalk with many women. I was trying to understand what was happening. I was having thoughts of being misplaced, remembering all the stories of sudden attacks—forcing people to run—some with bundles, some with nothing—not even family.

I have been trying to get back to sleep for what must be about an hour now.

The roosters are screaming.

This place seems to echo noises. I can hear footsteps and floors creaking. I can hear the noises of some animal, but I can't identify it, maybe a monkey.

I try to close my eyes a little longer.

Today is Sunday and not much happens until after prayers.

I just came back from a walk. I decided after breakfast I would take some time to see where I am. I was told this area is safe.

As soon as I was outside I put away my sunglasses. Even though the sun was blaring, I felt safer if people could see my eyes. They might feel I am not a threat.

Also, I did not want to flash anything of value, not because I feared theft, but because I felt bad. I walked around people who were living with so little.

Very soon my feet and pants were covered in red dirt.

One of the UNHCR security guards, a Sierra Leonean named William, asked if he could show me the area (the army barracks and the hospital). I immediately agreed.

We started up the road and ran into George.

For over a year, George has been working at UNHCR cooking breakfast and dinner. It is a good job, but it still doesn't provide enough money to take care of himself, let alone his family.

But he was not complaining. The only thing both of these men expressed was how beautiful this place once was. At one time, all of the people were good to everyone. Now everyone suffers. They hope life here will one day be good again, but it's hard to keep up hope or believe that one day it truly will get much better.

I asked George about his family. He said his mother just arrived from a refugee camp in Guinea. I asked if she was okay. He said she is better now, but she still gets colds, because where she now lives, she has to sleep on the floor.

George was taken by the rebels. He said, "They came at night. We all tried to run. My mother was so worried about me."

George has three children. "One I have not met," he said.

We walked by the hospital. It is a very old, small building with the paint almost completely removed.

There are two Red Cross tents. I would guess about five cots could fit in each tent. Maybe the reason there were no cots at all was more people could fit on the floor.

Many people are out walking around today—most in what

must be their Sunday best—colorful and clean. I don't know how they manage to have nice clothes, but this Sunday tradition is important to them. It is so beautiful to see.

We continued to walk the dirt road passing rocks, water, and streams of what I assume—by the awful smell—to be sewer water.

I could hear chanting and drumming. William and George pointed and said, "Church!"

The church was a small cement building with rubble around it. I looked inside and saw so many colorful silhouettes moving to the rhythm of the beating drum. Such beautiful people in prayer!

Since I have been here, this is the first time that I started to cry. I kept it to myself and walked on.

Little children walked by me. I smiled at them, and in return they smiled the sweetest, biggest smiles I've ever seen.

One little boy asked in a very serious tone—defiantly— "Who are you?"

"Angie."

He giggled, smiled, and walked away.

Saint Michael's Lodge UNICEF and Family Home Movement (FHM)

A little baby was put into my arms. No words could express how I felt.

Later, a small child put my hand into another woman's hand (an NGO American worker).

UNHCR is working with FHM to help those returning Sierra Leonean children who have been separated from their families.

A young African man was helping to manage the place. He was very nurturing to the others, very much a leader and a caregiver. He had very kind eyes.

I asked him questions as one would to get to know somebody. What does he love? Who is his family? I wanted to know who he was.

He does have family. Many of his brothers and sisters are at the university in Italy. He likes to travel, but he feels he can do good and is needed there.

He said he does have a few months' leave coming up, and he would like to take courses in counseling trauma victims. He wants to help orphans, and refugee children, and child soldiers with their traumas. This need is often overlooked.

"Maybe they expect them to just bounce back."

He explained to me how in other parts of the world—when someone needs help—counseling is available.

It is different in Africa. Hopefully, you are helped and supported by entering or joining a community.

I met a boy who had just been fitted with a prosthetic leg. He was standing listening to news on a small radio. People tell me he is one of the brightest students. He is already walking well.

A boy of about eleven high-fived the nun showing us around. "Sistah!"

UNHCR, along with Saint Michael's, is trying to help register and track families—reuniting them.

There is hardly any international news here. You only hear of the horrors nearby.

If only the wars and the worst of the people here are being reported, then people hesitate to invest in building up Africa. It is such an overwhelming problem. What do you do? People here become dependent and don't want to leave the refugee camps. I can understand why. Their homeland is still dangerous and empty. There is no food at home. There are no jobs at home.

Since it was Sunday and we had a day off, at the end of the day we drove to the water. The beaches here are so white! What a beautiful sight—white sand, light blue water surrounded by mountains covered in lush green!

This land was named Sierra Leone, because as the first settlers arrived at these shores, it was said to be thundering (like roaring lions).

Monday, February 26— 7 A.M. Breakfast Talk

Everyday it seems I learn more and more. In the countries with no diamonds, the people are not getting their hands on good weapons.

Some governments or individuals are getting richer trading with the RUF.

The United States and more countries in Europe should help the Sierra Leone Army, just like the British Army and S.A.S. are currently helping by training the Sierra Leoneans to defend themselves against the rebels.

FAWE—Forum for African Women Educationalists

Girls are educated and taught skills. They are being helped to be independent.

Most of these young women were abducted and raped.

I went into a small room.

Two women were looking after about ten babies.

Many of the women got pregnant when raped.

The babies didn't have toys or soft, colored things.

They were on the floor. Beautiful faces.

As I approached, one baby started crying, almost screaming.

The women apologized and said, "He's scared because of the color of your skin."

When I was in the classroom I was introduced as the Good Will Ambassador with UNHCR. Maya, the woman with me, was introduced as the protection officer with UNHCR.

All the young women were very welcoming.

It was then explained to them that I am also an actress from California. The woman who runs the school told them I was there to learn about them so I can support their programs.

They hardly know any movies. I hadn't wanted it brought up, but it did seem that my being an actress made my visit more fun for them. What I do is a strange job for them to imagine doing.

Sometimes being an actress seems strange to me too, but I was happy about it today.

After spending some time together we began to communicate even without an interpreter. Creole is a little like very fast, condensed English.

They asked me for my address. I thought for a moment about maintaining my privacy as I have been told to do in the States, but they shared with me, and so I will share with them.

I want so much for these young girls to succeed. I also want to be a friend. I went to the chalkboard and wrote my name and my private address.

One girl held my hand and said slowly, "I would like to be your friend."

She wrote her name down so I could recognize her letter.

Jui Transit Centre

Jui Transit Centre is situated at the mouth of the capital of Sierra Leone, just some seven miles to the heart of the capital city, Freetown. Established in 2000, Jui Transit Centre was one of the temporary settlements which were primarily put in place by the UNHCR in Freetown in response to the large-scale repatriation of Sierra Leonean refugees in Guinea. Following alleged Sierra Leonean RUF rebel cross-border attack on Guinea, Guineans swooped on Sierra Leonean refugees, who were accused of harbouring RUF rebels and trying to destabilise Guinea. Many Sierra Leonean refugees were physically manhandled, forcing many to opt for a return to Sierra Leone even though the war in their country of origin was still raging. As a large part of the country then was under rebel occupation, the returnees could not return to their villages. To meet the returnees' need for temporary accommodation, UNHCR established two host communities (Lokomassama and Barri) in the northern and southern provinces. However, as returnees arrived by ship from Guinea, there was need for them to stay overnight not just to recuperate after a long journey but also to make decisions on where they will proceed based on the information they received about other family members. In Jui, like in other transit centres, returnees were provided with such services. In principle, returnees were to stay for no more than five days in the Transit Centre, but in reality, some 2,000 returnees were sheltered at the centre until June 2002.

The Transit Centre itself is a neigbour to the Jui Village, which is home to an estimated 6,000 Sierra Leoneans. There is a primary school and a secondary school as well as a Bible Training Institute. Returnees had to send their children to these schools while they were at the centre. The Transit Centre itself had a health post, a huge water bladder with several water collection points.

Plastic tents, dirt floors. It feels like nowhere. People walk around. Can't help themselves. Can't go home.

A man ran up to UNHCR workers, his hardworking hands begging for them to come quick.

They explained that he wanted them to look at a boy.

I met the boy. He looked about twelve, but he could have been sixteen. It is hard to tell because of the malnourishment. He was very sick.

I didn't want to lean over and look. I kept a distance. I was a woman he didn't know. He was being examined by a doctor.

He was so young and yet seemed so aware of what was happening to him. His legs had become paralyzed. His stomach and his ribs seemed too wide. Later, I was told it looked as if he had been operated on. His spine was severely damaged. Disease was eating away at his body. It is likely this all began with a gunshot wound and a poor operation.

Here he was being released from the hospital. There are no funds and there is no room to care for him past what is considered an emergency (by their standards).

To me, this was an emergency. Now the humanitarian workers will try to look for help—but this boy is one of millions like him.

I will never be able to forget his face. I will never forget the way he moved his legs with his hands.

UNHCR is in Africa to help these persecuted people, and to continue to support the many needs of these refugees. There is always a concern of running out of funding for all of the necessary programs.

I sat with leaders and chiefs and young women who live in the camps.

I asked, "What do you want people to know?"

A young woman answered, "We continue to live in fear. We are scared of more girls being abducted and raped. We are scared of our young boys being taken off to war. We need this war to end."

A UNHCR worker asked, "Do you think America can help?"

The young woman quickly responded, "Yes, they are a

superpower! We want to go home. Our children need to go to school. We need proper food."

If only America were the place they think it is. It could be.

Someone asked the elder chief, "How does it feel in a camp?"

"We are embarrassed."

I have been told the funding is decreasing as UNHCR is attempting to expand. Countries of asylum are now having problems—countries like Guinea.

UNHCR is now handling internally displaced persons (IDPs) as well as refugees.

So many other organizations are set for long-term funding. UNHCR is set up only temporarily. They can't count on long-term funding; therefore, it is difficult to create strong and lasting solutions.

They really don't know if their programs will continue to be funded in the months to come, and yet there seem to be more people in need than ever. The problem (the need) is not going away.

I met a UNHCR man from Jordan. He spoke of building a FAWA-type center for women in refugee camps or settlements in his area.

Waterloo (Transit Centre)

The children here grab your hands and walk with you, smiling and singing. They have nothing. They are wearing ripped dusty clothes and they are smiling.

The children came running. They are so happy to have what little they have now. They are no longer alone or in fear for their safety. Most of them had to walk many, many miles for days with no food or water.

Their tiny little hands grabbed on to mine. There was a child's hand around every finger of mine. More children grabbed on to my wrists—my arms. It was nearly impossible for me to walk. I wanted to take each and every one of them home with me.

They saw my tattoos. They found them funny. They asked, "Who stamped you?"

A woman told me her story. As she was talking she unwrapped her grandchild from her back and began to breastfeed the baby. Her daughter (the child's mother) had been suspected of being a rebel in Guinea because of her tribal tattoos. She was killed.

Suddenly, one of the men I came with stood in front of me with his hand out. "Time to go. Get up, please."

I could hear fighting.

It was an argument about moving to another camp. A refugee did not want to leave.

I've been told some refugees demand that they be sent to a certain camp, because they think they might find their family members there.

We made our way past the argument to the car.

I noticed a man hitting a wall.

My companion shouted, "Lock your door!"

I did not feel frightened. I felt sad for the people in the

camps as well as for the UNHCR workers, who are unable to fulfill all the needs of all the refugees. When the refugees are upset, the UNHCR workers sometimes get the blame. These are workers affected by war victims.

It is hard to be prepared when the number of refugees and situations are always changing. So many people need help to stay alive. Many children going to school need medical attention—immunizations.

There are 22 million refugees. Two months ago I had no idea.

We need to help those who have to run to escape to survive.

Problems and numbers will only increase until we stop these wars.

Many of the children in the Waterloo Camp have scabies. I would rather get infected than to ever think about pulling my hands away from these little children.

The bigger realization is that this is only one of the many things these children are living with. The visible conditions are not good. To be honest, they are awful. I'm sure most of the worst atrocities are not even visible.

I just walked back into the room where I sleep. I washed my face and hands. I found myself staring at my hands.

Later that day, I went to an amputee camp full of internationally displaced persons supported by other nongovernmental organizations.

I have just been holding the pen in that spot for the last few minutes.

I don't know what to write. No—yes, I do. I am angry. I hate the people who did this. I hate that everyone is suffering—the amputees, the refugees, the displaced persons, the people living in their war-torn community—everyone. There are so many surviving while loved ones have been maimed or killed. No one is living as they did before the RUF. I don't understand how it continues—how my country can claim it comes to the aid of these countries in need when all the people here live every day knowing there has been no justice, no vengeance, and no real peace.

And how do you tell these refugees to start to rebuild their lives when they are sure that the rebels will just take it away again?

A man told me the story of how he lost his arm (from the elbow down). "The lucky ones are amputated. We are left alive—but not all of us—many amputees die from loss of blood or infection."

The youngest amputee I met was a little one-year-old girl. She was three months old when they cut off her arm and raped her mother.

So many people.

A young man I was sitting with for a while told me his story. He was a businessman. "I sleep on the floor. I don't have enough food. I am grateful I am alive, but I can never go home. How will I ever trade again?"

It was the look in his eyes that I can't forget—shaky, desperate, traumatized.

A man with no hands understood I was there to try to help. (I was introduced as a woman from America who is here to bring information back to the U.S.)

I have never wanted to succeed at anything more in my life.

The man with no hands put his arm out and smiled at me. I shook his wrist.

I felt humbled to be among such brave people.

Dinner at the UNHCR House

Tonight we had fish and salad.

It was a big luxury. I was grateful but I had trouble eating. I felt so hollow.

Protection officers joined us. For two and a half hours we talked about problems. Everyone shared different projects they are working on or serious events they have witnessed.

So much was discussed—too much for me to write—and everything is always well documented by UNHCR.

A man from Jordan said, "With love and tolerance anything is possible."

It's such a beautiful feeling to sit with different workers from all over the world—different ages, sexes, nationalities—all with different stories of why they are working with UNHCR.

Some UNHCR workers were once refugees themselves.

They spoke about the boy I saw at the Jui Transit Centre. Another person commented, "The boy with the peaceful face." "Maybe it wasn't a gunshot wound." "Maybe he fell very far."

One woman said, "He won't make it."

I shouldn't have been surprised by that, but I was.

A number of cases in the camps will die without proper hospital care. We need to push for more approval from Geneva (UNHCR). This all takes time.

It was explained to me that in the camps there are other victims who are not often discussed. I have never read or heard about what they revealed to me. Many refugees were forced to cut people. A gun is put to their head or a knife is put in their side. They are handed rusted swords or sharp glass. They are forced to cut hands, feet, or complete arms and legs off people they know—quite often family members.

These people are going mad. They are no longer able to function. In many cases, it becomes impossible for them to live with the guilt. There is hardly any counseling for them. There are barely enough funds for physical survival, let alone help for their mental and emotional recovery.

I can see how the refugees all try very hard to look after each other.

I want to write something before I go to bed. But I can't; I'm in shock.

Tuesday, February 27

There was a loud wake-up knock at my door. It is 7 A.M. Today I am tired. I was worried I might have disturbing dreams. So I am glad that I slept so hard. I didn't dream at all.

I sat in the office for about two and a half hours, going over information and having meetings to understand the different organizations.

Today, we are meeting a boat that is bringing refugees back to Sierra Leone. Then we will drive them to a camp near Kenema that will become their new home.

The boat was late. Finally, a call came in. "Time to move!" I grabbed my backpack. Another half hour passed. We were handed a small bag of basic camp equipment. "In case you break down. . . ."

Our car was in the garage all morning for maintenance. It's not much of a garage. The car is still not ready.

Everything here takes very long. The registration of the refugees coming off the boat is taking a while as well.

Many government and nongovernmental organizations were there at the dock, three or four people from each group.

- International Medical Corps
- Red Cross
- Save the Children
- UNHCR
- World Vision
- International Organization for Migration

Since the time I woke up this morning, the refugees have been waiting at the docks in the hot sun, getting whatever food can be supplied (a small loaf of bread and sardines).

I asked how long the boat ride would be for them this morning.

"Eleven hours!"

Even though the sea was calmer than usual, many children were throwing up. Two hundred and two people were counted.

A woman walked there today to meet the boat. She is looking for her husband. He was not there. She was told to check at registration. It's a small table in the corner of the dock. The only spot out of the sun.

As we drive through the streets at the start of our five-hour journey, at almost every stop beggars come up to the windows.

There were blind and injured children—children severely handicapped for life. I asked if it was all right to give money. "No, not in this public area. Everyone will come. It sets a bad precedent."

There are over 200 people on this journey. Behind us are two small trucks carrying all their belongings. These two small U-Haul-type trucks contain the lifetime possessions of over 200 people. They contain all they have in the world.

I don't know how the people in the trucks are coping after all they have been through just with this journey from Guinea. I can't imagine what it was like when they were running. How did they make it to Guinea in the first place?

We picked up more refugees in Waterloo. The count is now 387 people.

We are driving back to town to buy what we can.

These people are coming home. They were refugees in Guinea, but now they are not safe there.

They are coming back to Sierra Leone to live in camps. Their homes were all destroyed. The areas they used to live in are now held by rebels.

They have no real choice but to live in camps with very little, and no real promise that the same people who destroyed their homes and killed and raped and maimed their family and friends will not attack again. But if they are going to die they want to die in their home country.

I can't imagine what they must be feeling.

They are packed in trucks and driven through the streets where they used to live free and happy.

Six trucks full of people.

Two smaller trucks with all their belongings.

We have been following in our truck for protection and support.

We have just moved ahead to lead the way. We are the only protection vehicle so every half hour we check everyone by moving from the front to the back.

We have just been informed that there is no water packed for the journey. A woman (a UNHCR officer) is trying to make contact by radio. It is a bad connection. She is asking how to find supplies along the way. We need to figure out the water supply.

We have also been told we will be arriving in the dark, because it has taken longer than expected to leave.

I was asked if I was still sure I wanted to go.

They said there is no reason to worry, but they would prefer if I got off one stop before the final one. They said it would make them more comfortable.

I don't want to put myself at unnecessary risk, because I understand UNHCR would feel responsible. We agreed to make a decision when we got there. We would also have to figure out where we can stay.

Another protection vehicle just joined the convoy. Our driver signaled for them to take the back.

UNHCR is also here to make sure they clear all roadblocks and checkpoints.

We are now driving through the area where the British helped to clear out the rebels.

The Westside Boys

The Westside Boys were a group of ex-soldiers who supported the military coup which ousted President Ahmad Tejan Kabbah in May 1997. They fled to the bush together with other soldiers of the Sierra Leone Army (SLA) when the Economic Community Monitoring Group (ECOMOG) reversed the coup in February 1998 and reinstated President Ahmad Tejan Kabbah.

The Westside Boys were part of the invading forces which captured over half of Freetown on 6 January 1999, when at least 5,000 people were killed and houses and properties estimated at millions of dollars were destroyed. The Westside Boys fled again to the bush when ECOMOG forces beat them back from the capital. Then, they stayed around Okra Hills situated about 50 km from Freetown.

They ambushed a number of civilian and military vehicles, causing a lot of disturbances along the Freetown-Masiaka Highway. The capture of some British military personnel and their Sierra Leonean SLA guide climaxed the activities of the Westside Boys. When all negotiations to secure the release of the captives proved futile, the British launched land-air operations, killing and capturing the Westside Boys in the jungle. Those who were captured, including the jungle leader, self-styled Brig. Foday Kallay, are all behind bars in Freetown. It was these operations which put the existence of the Westside Boys to an end. The Westside Boys named themselves after one of the gangster groups in the United States, the Westside Squad.

Now we are on another road, but this road is not good. We need to go east. Our arms are out the windows, signaling the trucks behind us to speed up.

I saw a man walking along the road. He was wearing shorts and was very dirty. He was holding a machine gun and he was yelling—talking to himself.

Shells of burnt-down houses are everywhere.

Cars and trucks must have exploded here as well, leaving only rusty turned-over shells.

Beautiful jungle.

Occasionally, I see small villages that are half burnt down and half built back up with wood and dirt (clay).

The few old schools and churches along this road appear empty and full of bullet holes.

If we arrive at the camp after 8 P.M., we won't be able to enter.

Many people were upset at how fast we had to drive. "Sorry. Secure your children. The sooner we get there, the sooner you can eat and rest. We do not want to travel too much in the dark."

They understood. Still, there seems to be no end to their difficult journeys. Even after today it is far from over. A little better maybe—still alive.

We are now about two and a half hours into our journey. One of the baggage trucks just broke down. Everything in it had to be unloaded and then reloaded into the second baggage truck. I don't see how they are going to fit everything into one truck. It seemed packed before.

We continue on while they transfer all the bags. They will try to catch up.

I will never be able to express or translate who these people are, what they are going through, or why it is so important that we help them.

I suggested that someone should organize a video camera so they can speak for themselves. They want very much to do that.

They don't want the press to decide what is important. They want to talk for themselves.

I thought when I came here I would be saddened and sickened by all that has happened to these people and how they are living.

Instead, I see their survival, their still smiling faces, kids holding hands, people (what seems to be everybody) working. I am in awe of these people.

Their will.

Their hope.

We stop to unload a few people in one area. The food seems to be in the truck that is far behind us—the baggage truck.

We are all sitting together outside. It is about two in the afternoon and the heat is unbearable. I see so many refugees working—carrying wood and other things, trying to settle this new area. I don't know how they do it.

Someone explained to me that morning is about getting supplies for breakfast (water, wood), eating, cleaning, and trying to sell or make things if they can.

Afternoon is about getting water and wood and making lunch.

It's the same at dinner.

All day is about survival.

UNHCR lost four staff members this year.

Every week, one humanitarian worker somewhere in the world is killed. There is a great need for much more safety and protection.

The UNHCR agency has one of the highest rates of divorce, suicide, and depression.

Entering Area 91 a sign reads:

PLEASE DO NOT CUT HANDS
LET'S JOIN HAND

We had to walk to a market to buy extra sardines and bread. Our supplies were only half the needed amount.

We are told a boy on the third truck is very sick. The nurse has very little medical supplies—none, really.

UNHCR needs so much more funding for doctors, nurses, and medicine. Operations are rarely performed smoothly here.

I am here with Nyambé, a UNHCR woman who has been accompanying me to my various appointments and activities. This is her first convoy and first visit to a camp not close to a transit center.

We went for medical supplies. We saw U.N. soldiers stationed in the area. It turns out they were from Bangladesh.

One of the soldiers did not want to help us. He said, "Go find NGOs." We looked back at the dusty roads, the poor townspeople, and the little shacks.

"Where?" we asked.

Nyambé explained that we are all brothers and sisters under the U.N. flag.

They asked if we were doctors.

We explained, "No, just workers."

They gave us a small bag with medicine for pain and dehydration.

After food is distributed, we check our bags.

Heads of families step forward for those not on the registration forms. A yellow paper card will allow a bread roll and a half can of sardines per person.

The sun is going down. We are trying to call ahead to get a place in the Bo camp, which is one hour closer, to prepare dry-food rations for 400 people.

We will not make it to our final destination. We will have to head out again in the morning.

We had a flat tire on the second (of the two) baggage

trucks. We have to move on as they change it. The first truck was left behind earlier in the day—mechanical problems.

UNHCR may have problems, but they are the only ones here to attempt this convoy.

No one is here taking pictures for CNN. It is just another day.

It is now 7:40 P.M. It is pitch-black outside. A man is walking toward us. He was from one of the trucks ahead of us. We pulled over.

"What's the problem?" we asked.

He said, "My truck has no headlights."

We are waved down at a checkpoint by young boys. They shine flashlights in our truck and hold the lights on our faces. They let us pass.

It is 9:30 P.M. We arrived at Bo. We will spend the night here and move on at 7 A.M.

We met with Muhammad, who was working there. He had prepared (with the others) three large bowls of bulgur wheat and three large bowls of beans.

We started to give out food with the woman who was clearly a leader of the group. It had already taken a while to unload all the refugees from the trucks, and everyone was very hungry.

I can't imagine how they were feeling. I was nauseous. I probably would have thrown up from the ride, but I did not have any liquids and I only ate bread for the last few hours. There was no bathroom along the journey so I drank no water.

I tried to help by handing out cups and spoons, and making sure that the servers had enough plates. There were not enough metal plates to go around, so we tried to organize washing when the first to eat were finished.

The children were fed first, then the women, and finally the men.

Some referred to me as *"pumwi,"* which means "white person."

Some called me "sistah."

They were very kind to me, aware I was there to help.

Other people might push and yell and be angry for all the time it had been taking and all they had been through.

But they have been through so much for years now and, if anything, I felt they were helping me to understand how it was done because I was new.

Nyambé and I were told to sleep in a nearby motel. It doesn't feel right that I am given this privilege, but I am so tired. I am deeply grateful.

They gave us rooms with fans, but mine is not working. Out the window I hear people talking and very obscure '80s American music. I just saw a fat jumping spider.

The bed board was once covered in plastic, but now it is mostly ripped off. There are no sheets on the bed, only a mattress cover.

I can't help but love this room. The man who took me to it smiled when the door opened and said, "Nice! Good!" Then he showed me the toilet and, with an even bigger smile, he said, "Look!" And then he flushed the toilet.

He just returned a moment ago to give me matches and a candle.

There is no electricity from 1 A.M. to 4:30 A.M.

Nyambé came into my room, and we split what was left of the loaf of bread. It was too hot to eat so I saved my share for breakfast.

Wednesday, February 28

6:17 A.M. We are back in line and almost ready to start toward Kenema.

I hardly slept. It was so hot and the noise was constant. I kept thinking about how much better I had it than the refugees. I thought of how the mothers and babies might feel at night. I wondered why so few children were crying. I suppose they are used to these awful conditions, or maybe they are just too tired to cry.

This morning I discovered a big knife slice in my door. Nyambé said she noticed it last night when she was knocking.

I wonder about privacy, but I don't really care. It is too early and I am happy to be on the road again.

Many people with UNHCR are from the countries they are working for so it feels like (and often is) their own people helping them. Communities and countries helping each other.

The Norwegian Refugee Council was also there to give support.

We finally arrived. Groups of people brought before on other trips ran out to see if they might recognize a friend or member of their family. A few people who had been traveling in the trucks screamed with joy when they recognized a friend. Each family group was given a plot of land to start building. They were given a small bundle of supplies.

The refugees need help to start projects that will make them independent.

It would be nice to have a workshop to teach them about gardening so they can grow their own food.

This new refugee area has only been in existence for a few weeks, and already there are many little clay and wooden hut structures that are built.

At the office I saw about seven people waiting with very large bundles. Some women were pregnant. I was told these women are among the hundreds of people who came from Guinea. They came on foot, and they need medical attention, registration, and placement in the camp.

We are at the airport waiting to be flown back. It is a small, white building surrounded by nearby army campsites.

African troops are wearing U.N. hats and their flag on their uniforms.

More British troops just arrived—in full uniform—carrying large sacks and guns. They all run in an orderly fashion as they disembark the helicopters and run to board the trucks.

We were told our plane was here, but it is not. So we wait—trying to stay out of the hot sun.

When the plane didn't come, we asked for an estimate. One hour. We all wanted breakfast, or at least coffee, so we decided to drive to a nearby café. It was little and dusty and great.

A strange mix of African and Chinese. The menus were old, and I could hardly make out the words. We ordered and started to discuss the various things each person was dealing with. But as soon as we started talking, two minutes after we ordered, we heard the plane had landed, and we had to run. We laughed.

The local airline was understandably late from all the military activity. About ten of us crammed in. It was hot. Some music was playing that I can't even describe. I think the words were in French. Once it started to play it never stopped.

When we finally made it back it was almost 2 P.M. On the drive in I watched the people. Now I have a better understanding of their struggles.

I look out the window.

The romance of their bravery falls shadow to the very little boy trying to support gallons of water on his head. He is barefoot. It is very hot and I am sure he has far to go. And long after I am gone—or as someone might be reading this—he will still be doing it, as well as many other things. He is just a little boy. And he is one of the lucky ones—for now. He is not in the army. He has access to water. No one has cut his hands or feet off. And although he is very skinny, he seems to be relatively healthy.

A photographer came into the office asking about what is happening in the different areas, and could he have help or information on how to get into the areas of most conflict right now.

It is difficult because it is hard to access most areas. It has been hard to even get food to people in need there.

They tried to work out a route and different rides along the way where he could hitch a ride. He is trying to help bring awareness so people can see what is happening and judge for themselves how they feel.

I am sure that most of the pictures he takes are images many of us don't want to see—but should.

He asked where I was from.

"America."

"Ah! I have been a photographer for ten years. American press don't buy these kinds of pictures. Other countries do."

Tonight I am scheduled to have dinner with Mr. Arnauld Akodjenou, the representative of UNHCR in Sierra Leone. He is going to help me understand what is going on in this country—what is being done, what needs to be done, and the politics.

I tried to clean the dirt off my boots and find clean pants. But I'm sure he understands. There was something nice about my clothes being so dirty and knowing why.

I don't feel I am able to help very much at all now, but I am starting to do something. And it feels very good to know, as time goes on, that I will be able to help more.

On my way to dinner I was told Mr. Akodjenou was going to be late. "There are problems. The police got wind of a demonstration tomorrow."

When I got to his home, I was led by a man with a flashlight.

His property had two-foot-high circles of barbed wire over the gates.

Inside, every window was secured. Different types of metal or plasterwork were used so as not to look like bars.

The more I learn about this man and the people here, the more I realize the risks they face.

Apparently, today was the end of the government term. Some people want to see a change in government. They want to take over. He is not sure exactly who will be demonstrating, but he mentioned probably some RUF.

The last time there was a demonstration, nineteen people lost their lives. On the day of that occurrence, he was stuck in his office. I think he said from 10 A.M. to 4 P.M. And when the vehicle was on its way to finally get him out—it was hijacked.

He told me it was suggested after the last demonstration that they should move the office. Other U.N. agencies had left the area, but their landlord would have held them to $55,000 for the agreed lease. They could not afford to move, and they did not feel it was as important as all the other things the money could be used for.

He spoke about his appreciation of the staff, who are so dedicated. They continue to work there, even though they know the dangers.

Also, in this country the staff cannot have family with them at this time. An emergency situation calling more of them to this area happened right after Christmas. Many have not seen their families in a very long time.

Tomorrow everyone will stay inside—everyone who can. Three people will have to make it to the wharf because refugees are coming again from Guinea. Buses will have to be rented. Trucks could be targeted because of the U.N.

I was supposed to help with registration, but I have been asked to please stay inside.

The American Embassy is one of the targets.

Nigeria, the United States, and England supported the past term and don't want a change.

I hope I am getting all these facts right.

I am frightened. I know everything will be fine, but I also must admit that because I don't know anything about these situations, I suppose anything can happen.

It may seem silly, but I think I will pack up my backpack before I fall asleep—just in case I wake up and have to run out. The good thing is I am exhausted, and I think I will be able to sleep.

Also, I am supposed to have a meeting tomorrow—a dinner with Joseph Melrose. He is the U.S. Ambassador to Sierra Leone. I will also be meeting with different NGOs as well.

I am not sure what will happen now. I don't really know what is going on.

Thursday, March 1

9:30 A.M. and no news.

A man came to hook up a better radio contact.

At breakfast we didn't talk about it at all.

We shared photos and stories about our families.

10:20. It looks like it may not happen. But no one will leave for the office for a few hours—just in case.

Maybe the fact that they were prepared to defend themselves stopped it. Apparently troops have been guarding different headquarters, offices, and embassies since early this morning.

I had to go into town to pick up money from Western Union.

Nyambé picked me up in her car so they could not see UNHCR on the work truck. Police stopped us and checked us.

We were at Western Union fifteen minutes early, but they would not let us in the office. They had strict orders. Most of the staff were leaning against the walls across the street.

In the UNHCR office we hear from men who were at the wharf that about 485 refugees arrived today. They will stay in a transit center until tomorrow, and then they will go up by convoy. This time they are going home.

We also hear that the demonstration will start at 3 P.M. Others say the police were already stopping them from assembling. The other rumor is that they will start demonstrating at the American embassy. I have an appointment there this afternoon.

We have tried calling to confirm my appointment with Ambassador Melrose, but we are told we have the wrong number. It must be for security reasons, because we checked and it is the correct number.

I did notice bullet holes in the glass inside the embassy. At some point, people were here to attack and they got inside. Luckily, there are many different levels to "inside."

There was tremendously high security at the U.S. embassy. I don't know why I thought it would be like visiting home. My country. It didn't feel that way at all. I was left outside as

Nyambé was interviewed and ID checked. Then I was signaled in. They wiped down my bag and put the swab in a computer. I also had to walk through a metal detector. Once I was inside, everyone was very friendly.

We discussed how there were about 400 amputees in the camp that I saw, and many more in the camps at Bo and Kenema. Most of them are staying together, but they have no support or funds.

I was told there are two new amputees. There had not been any at all in the last year. It had stopped. But around Ramadan, a child about one and a half and another about eight had received fresh wounds.

Their hands were cut off.

We sat in silence for a moment. Then the ambassador said, "It is very sad. There are always things that need to be done."

I later sat in on a meeting on how to fix some of the convoy problems to help it run smoother. With lack of funds they have to shift things around. They depend on NGOs and other U.N. agencies to help in time.

They have to make adjustments and compromises. The lives of many people are affected by every decision, and they all hurt every time something is cut back.

The number of arriving refugees is so high—400 a day. Can we handle more? Where can we place them?

These refugees are already sharing their food rations. They are feeling so overcrowded. They are not welcoming new arrivals. It's not that it's their choice, but they will fight new arrivals for food. It sounds harsh, but it is survival.

As everyone talks, I notice their frustration and their fight to find solutions.

There is no air conditioner so they open the windows. Everyone now has to talk very loudly because we are on a street with many trucks passing by.

Behind me there is a table with four photographs of the UNHCR staff workers who were killed in the line of duty in 2000. They look like very kind people. Sweet faces.

I had a wonderful dinner with Joseph Melrose. Other NGO officials were also there—most of them working for UNHCR. We talked all night about the different countries and situations.

We also managed to be very human and share some laughs. I don't know what I should or should not write about. There were many different opinions. I can write that I felt everyone in the room was very dedicated to finding solutions.

To understand or explain the RUF, or how and when they will be dealt with, is very difficult. Everyone seemed in agreement that they did not trust that the RUF had really granted "safe passage" from Guinea to Sierra Leone—through their territory. I had wondered myself why the rebels would do that.

To steal supplies?

To take hostages?

To make human shields?

There is nothing else in it for them, so why would they?

There is no answer.

There is a lot of funding for the refugees, but the majority is earmarked for areas where some projects are already well supported. Some camps have more than enough while other areas have hardly anything.

The organizations do not have the right to move that money around.

The amputees have had much support and press. It is wonderful people cared and stepped up with funds.

But as I understand it more now, many of the war wounded—even many of the amputees—were not all victims tortured directly by the rebels. I have been told that many doctors were forced at gunpoint by the rebels to do some of the cutting and mutilating. If they didn't obey these brutal, inhuman orders, the doctors and their families would be killed.

The camps for the war-wounded areas definitely need more funding.

As I sit here writing, it is hard to believe that I will be leaving Sierra Leone tomorrow.

Friday, March 2

I am on a plane leaving Freetown, Sierra Leone, flying to Abidjan, Côte d'Ivoire (for one night).

I don't know what I am feeling.

A woman who was traveling with her daughter thanked me for coming. "It is nice for us to know we are thought of." She was working with UNHCR and had also been in Guinea.

I wanted to thank her for her strength. I wanted to thank this country for allowing me to come here to learn as much as I have about such an amazing place and people.

But I couldn't speak. I was afraid I might cry.

As I was leaving Sierra Leone people said, "Please stay in touch. I hope you don't forget about us here." It was said with smiles—friendly. Of course I will never forget, but many people do.

There are places all over the world that need assistance. I was even surprised to hear of the problems in Ethiopia. I was under the impression that the situation in that country was better. I thought the worst was over because years ago so many stories of worldwide relief were in our news. Money and much awareness regarding Ethiopia was raised, and then it all seemed to go away. What I am reminding myself is that these problems do not disappear just because we do not hear about them. And in that thought—there is so much more happening around the world than what is communicated to us about the top stories we do hear.

We all need to look deeper and discover for ourselves. . . .

What is the problem?

Where is it?

How can we help solve it?

As we were getting off the plane, the pilot told us there had been an explosion in Conakry, the capital of Guinea.

Accident or attack?

We don't know.

Many people on the plane had just come from Conakry. It is where the plane originally departed from this morning. They had been warned that an attack may be coming.

Suddenly, all of us who had just been talking, and been happy to have arrived, were now sitting in silence. We walked out of the plane very slowly.

I am now waiting in passport control. Many people are on their cellular phones. I don't know what they are saying, because their conversations are in French—but it is obvious there is a reason for deep concern.

Finally, I was told that part of the army's ammunition depot blew up.

It doesn't sound like people were hurt.

It is hours later and I am alone. I feel sick. I don't know if I ate bad food or if I am upset.

Even though I am in a hotel tonight, I haven't been able to get through to home yet. I left a message and found myself crying.

I am very worried about everything I have seen. And I realize that if I am scared, how do these brave women manage when they are forced to flee their homes because of the war? Some of these women have not seen their husbands or their children in years. I can't stop thinking of all their different faces.

I am also remembering that young boy with the sweet face who has severe spinal damage. He will never walk again. I am resting in a hotel, and he is still in the corner on that dusty dirt floor.

I never cried when I was in Sierra Leone. With everything I saw, I never cried. Tonight I can't seem to stop crying.

Tomorrow I will see new faces. Tomorrow I have to do more.

I don't want to write anymore. I feel nauseous.

Saturday, March 3

I am on my way to Zurich, Switzerland. My next stop is Tanzania, but I can't fly there from the Ivory Coast so I will stay in Zurich for two nights. There must have been five security checkpoints. Everyone's bags were inspected with flashlights on the tables near the runway. Our bodies were inspected with metal detectors. I wonder what the security worry is.

Sunday, March 4

Here in Zurich, I am staying at the Dolder Grand Hotel on the lake.

Everything smells like oranges and vanilla.

There is snow on the ground.

I saw a young boy in the lobby and thought of the dusty little African boy carrying water on his head, sweating and trying so hard to focus.

Both innocent, cute, little boys just in separate parts of the world, and they will grow up so differently.

What decides where we are born and into what kind of life and why?

I can't stop sleeping. I didn't realize I was so tired.

Monday, March 5—8:40 P.M. Swissair Flight 292

I departed from Zurich bound for Dar es Salaam, Tanzania.

Tuesday, March 6

Before sunrise we prepared to board the second plane, but there was no paging system so we weren't sure what time the plane was going to take off.

While waiting to board I was casually making new introductions when a UNHCR worker came rushing toward me. . . . "We have to run!" The man who took our tickets gave us a scolding for being late. I kept apologizing. I thought he wasn't going to let us on.

It was a very old propeller plane. A flight that would normally have taken thirty minutes took three hours. We landed on a dirt road in the middle of the most beautiful green land. The sun was out.

Next was a two-and-a-half-hour drive to the headquarters near the refugee camp. I was told to put on my seatbelt "so you don't bounce around so much."

It is a holiday today. I am not sure what it is for or about, but any reason to celebrate seems like a good idea here.

Some say they don't understand why, with hardly enough food or supplies to survive, people sell their goods to buy impractical things, all for a wedding or a birthday. You realize that is what they are surviving for. They don't save up and wait for a magical day to come when it will all be better. They have to live each day for each day, as we all should.

We arrived not sure where we were staying or if there was any food for us anywhere.

We went to a market. I felt bad because I could buy food.

The market was so dirty and poor. I was worried about the health conditions. If the food was safe to eat. I bought bananas and a loaf of bread a man had made.

It is hard to keep seeing people so used to living in such poverty.

A man was making sandals out of old tires.

Suddenly, I looked up and saw a man whose hands were tied to a goat. A crowd of what must have been forty people, including children, were following him. They were surrounding him on both sides. He looked bloody and worn out. I realized some people were holding sticks. Someone hit the man on the back. The crowd cheered. Children were smiling. They hit him again. I felt sick.

I found the man I was with. "They are hitting that man. What are they doing? What's going on?"

He looked at them as they passed, and he asked a local man nearby to explain.

"He stole a goat and they are taking him to the police."

We decided to walk back.

We talked about the law. We talked about how sometimes it is better to handle things in a community or with "tribal law," but that sometimes this way is really a problem.

Even the man I was with had never seen this before—a thief punished that way.

I am now at the field officer's apartment (or compound, as they call it). The field officer's name is Alexandra; she lives in one of the homes on the compound. It is very modest, just what you need—a bed and a radio.

It had been sprayed for mosquitoes. A very strong smell remained in the room.

She told me not to brush my teeth with the water. It can be muddy and brown. It is safe to shower in though.

She went out with a few others. They left a walkie-talkie. "Just in case you need help—call 5354." They weren't kidding, but I also knew they would not have left me alone if they were really worried.

The thing is—if there is something that worries me—I doubt I will be rational enough to call.

I checked to see where she keeps her knives.

But I knew even after I grabbed one for security, I would just run.

Wednesday, March 7

I awoke to the sound of loud trucks, roosters, and birds.

Voices seemed to be right outside my window. There is just a screen so everything that passes is very loud. I don't know what language I am hearing. I listened as the sun came up. Then there was a knock, meaning it was time to get up.

Some refugee camp officers work seven days a week, alternating every two months. Many UNHCR staff members in the deep field end up working over weekends, although they are not official working days, due to the demanding and constant nature of the refugee protection and assistance work. VARI (Voluntary Absence for the Relief of Isolation) is intended to address cumulative stress for international staff who are posted in very remote and isolated duty stations. An unusual combination of extreme factors would need to exist, necessitating the periodic relief of mental and physical stresses present in the work environment. Internationally recruited staff take turns to go on a five-day VARI after working for two months in any of those duty stations. MARS (Mandatory Absence for the Relief of Stress) applies to those serving in more stressful and hazardous areas.

Alexandra and I talked over breakfast. We had coffee with dehydrated milk (as usual) and bread. She was happy to be able to offer me jam.

Alexandra told me about a three-year-old girl who was raped.

UNHCR is working on the laws to see to it that the man is punished. It takes years to get justice for these children. As they say, it is all so "very frustrating."

Nyarugusu Camp (Congo Refugees)

We traveled on an already very bad dirt road that has been made worse by all the rain. So many people were stuck on their way to the Nyarugusu camp.

Fifty-three-thousand refugees, all from the Congo, are here for food distribution that is brought in two times a month.

There are 250 births here every month.

All lost tribal members are brought here. Families are reunited.

The numbers are always growing.

Food rations are continually being cut down because of lack of funds. Everyone gets less than usual.

The system is very complex.

My first job was to work chute number 4, helping to pass large bags in bulk to groups.

I was focused on families of five. The children ranged in age from one to ten years old.

We were not able to distribute any cooking oil because the truck bringing it to the camp was stuck on a washed-out road.

I had lunch with members of Christian Outreach Relief and Development (CORD).

We had cabbage, water, rice, and beans. I was starving.

Local refugees who made instruments wanted to perform for us.

While we ate, we could hear the music.

I saw one little boy about three or four years old who climbed a tree to see inside the crowd.

There exists a refugee youth program in this camp that is run by UNHCR.

There would normally be about 200 more children than I saw during my visit, but it is food-distribution day.

The children I did meet were so warm and welcoming. They began to dance. I was told, "They could easily dance all day." At one point, I was signaled to dance with them. I did. The children seemed to find me extremely amusing.

Then it was explained to the audience that many refugee children, along with members of UNHCR, CORD, and myself, were going to perform a play about HIV and AIDS.

During the play, an AIDS-awareness worker handed the kids condoms and told them, "You have to use them if you don't get a blood test. Testing and condoms are available at all youth centers."

Three young men with streaks of white paint in their hair and made-up old man faces come out limping using wood sticks for canes. Everyone laughed to hear them complaining and acting like sick old men.

It was all so beautiful to see.

In the story, one man has a daughter who he wants to be careful about dating a certain boy. He wants her to stay home. She goes out with the boy anyway. Later, she finds out that another girl who had slept with that boy has AIDS.

In the camp, the refugees design and print AIDS-awareness T-shirts. They gave me one. The children laughed when I began putting my T-shirt over my head and it got stuck. They all clapped and hugged me when I finally managed to get it on.

Our next stop was where men were building large structures with mud and bricks. I tried to help for a little while, but I found it to be very hard work.

I told one of the workers how I admired him for being able to work there every day, all day long. He said, "Yes, it is hard work, but it is for the children, so it feels good."

As I write this, we are driving on a dirt road that has just become blocked by a tractor. The tractor is pulling a bus that was stuck in the mud earlier today and is stuck again.

All the children lined up to watch. They are laughing. It looks like the bus is a lost cause.

People are climbing out of the bus windows and walking into the bush. Some stayed to make money pushing the bus.

Then, as we tried to drive around the bus, we got stuck in the mud. Another tractor eventually came and got us out.

There was a hitchhiker on the road. Our driver told him, "Sorry, we can't carry people with weapons."

That was certainly not a normal thing you would hear someone saying to a hitchhiker in the United States!

I am watching the refugees. I have begun talking and dancing with them. I feel I am making friends.

Someone once said, "You can learn more about someone in an hour of play than in a year of conversation."

I experienced something like that—of the same nature. And that is what I felt.

They asked for my address. We promised to keep in touch.

The sad thing is they know they will not be leaving the camp anytime soon.

But the spirit of these people, and their will to survive, continues to amaze me. I wish I could find a better word. I am inspired by them. I am honored to spend time with them.

I am back in the room where I sleep.

I am exhausted and very dirty.

The hot water here comes from solar power, and the sun is not out, so the shower will be cold.

It is also getting dark, and no lights come on until 7:30 P.M.

There is no electricity from 12 A.M. to 7:30 A.M. or from 4 P.M. to 7:30 P.M.

Alexandra and I laughed, "The things we take for granted!"

She's right. And as much as today has been a hard day, it

felt very good. Being with these people in this country has made today one of the best days of my life.

But I remember I am only here for a short time. And I have a choice. I live very far away—comfortably.

I admire all of the people who work here—all of them.

Dark circles are under most of their eyes. They talk non-stop about how to solve problems—how better to help.

Sometimes—like tonight—they talk about the things they have seen.

The 1994 Genocide in Rwanda

Hundreds of thousands of refugees were walking over a bridge that connects Rwanda and Tanzania. The river below them was full of dead bodies—over 40,000 bodies. They tried to pull out as many as they could. Now it is a large burial ground.

Apparently, in 1994, England and the United States supported these people in their desire to go back home. It was believed there was now peace in Rwanda.

Even though they knew they were going home, many of them felt forced. While they trusted no harm would come to them, it was not like the voluntary repatriation that is happening in Sierra Leone.

But it was not safe to go back to Rwanda. There was no peace.

During the genocide, millions of people died.

But they all would rather die at home.

Alexandra helped me heat up a little vegetables and rice.

She is staying in tonight. She is tired. She has been traveling from one place to the next. She is looking forward to her seven days off.

They have an option of going to Dar es Salaam in Tanzania or to Nairobi in Kenya. I thought, when I heard about the seven days out of isolation, they would go home, or at least to a place that most people would truly call out of isolation.

But Alexandra is happy to be near an office. She still has work to do.

She will be happy to go to a market and buy supplies and food.

I am so spoiled. I have only been gone three weeks, and I have eaten more during my stops between countries than the refugees ever get to eat. And I can't wait to get to a market and to all the other luxuries of home.

Most of all, I can't wait to be able to be with my family, to know they are not in danger, and that they have everything they need.

I can't imagine what a mother or father or even a husband or wife feels when the people they love most in the world are suffering, and there is nothing they can do. . . .

When a mother can't feed a child.

When a father can't provide for his family.

When a husband can't protect his wife.

Alexandra spent today making birth certificates for the over 400 babies she looks after who have been born in the camps. She works with the Red Cross, making it official.

It is only about 8 P.M. but I am going to try to sleep soon.

Not even because I am tired, but because there is nothing to do to keep me awake. I have already read everything I brought with me. I noticed Alexandra's books on her shelf are from Holland. I can't read them.

It is now two and a half hours after writing the above. Now I am going to get ready for bed.

Alexandra and I spent that time talking about everything, even the dangerous situations she has been in because of her work.

Sleeping with clothes and boots on, ready to run.

Alexandra's friend was one of the men who was killed—slaughtered—while working for UNHCR.

We also discussed the major shortage and how they have no soap now for the refugees.

From now on, rations would be cut by 20%.

World Food Program (another U.N. agency responsible for food distribution) also has cutbacks.

It's nobody's fault, but it is frustrating, and hard to explain to people who are just getting by with what is already thought to be the bare necessities: the basic nutritional supplements to remain healthy and the right amount of calories to stay alive. Now it has to be about 80 percent of that amount, and still, they are lucky to have that.

We also talked about the women having no sanitary pads and what that must be like.

And Alexandra told me that in prisons here they have it worse. That they are locked in to live like animals and can't even clean themselves.

Thursday, March 8

Woke up to rain—a damp, cold day.

The roads, the food distribution, what happens to the camps when it rains?

I was scheduled to be picked up by a private studio plane on Saturday, because I had to do press and a premiere back home. I just got the news that no plane is coming because the premiere is cancelled.

You've got to love Hollywood.

This was going to be my way home.

I have hardly any supplies left—very little medicine, cash, and clean clothes.

I have no idea how to get back to L.A.

There are only eight-seater planes out of here every few days, and even then, they have long stopovers. Even with short-distance flights, what should be a scheduled one-hour layover, quite often ends up being one day. They tried to find a seat for me on tomorrow's flight, but the plane is full. I have to fly to Zurich and Amsterdam in order to get to L.A.

UNHCR will continue to try to help me from their office in Dar es Salaam, but they are very busy with much more important things to do.

No need for me at a premiere, and suddenly, it's "find your own way home."

Mtabila Camp

95,000 refugees here (mostly Burundians).

UNHCR brought me to the nutritional and medical center, which is run inside the camp by the Red Cross.

My first job today was measuring the medicine powder at the therapeutic feeding center.

Under the age of five—extra nutrition.

Pregnant—measured.

I wanted to be careful not to measure a spoonful too short.

They have to monitor the children to make sure they are growing and not losing weight. The newborns are measured for height and weight and given vaccines. One little baby was scared and peed on the examining table. The mother used part of her dress to wipe it off. There is no soap available. Keeping safe and clean is very hard for everyone.

The kitchen contains a very small room with three large clay pots on wood-burning stoves.

It was hard to see. All the smoke in the room hurts my eyes.

I helped make milk for the mothers. It comes dehydrated in bulk. With a small plastic pitcher I took two liters of boiling hot water (I measured the best I could) and poured it into an old beaten-up green plastic bucket. It's hard not to let the hot water burn your hands.

You leave it in the bucket until it cools down (so it won't destroy the milk proteins), then you mix it.

Pediatric Ward

There were about fifteen small wooden beds lined up on each side of the room. Nets surrounded each bed—to try to prevent mosquito bites that can lead to malaria. Most of the nets have holes in them. Malaria is very common in this area, almost impossible to avoid. Another big problem is diarrhea. To babies and small children the loss of bodily fluids is deadly.

I have deet spray on at all times, and still I have been bitten by mosquitoes—and not just at night. I am also very lucky to have malaria pills. The pills don't stop you from getting malaria, but they help prevent the severity of it if it comes.

An eight-year-old was sitting with her baby brother on her lap.

They were sitting on the last bed. She had him wrapped up. The baby had lost 200 grams. He has diarrhea and he also might have worms.

This little girl saw her parents and her older brother brutally killed. Somehow she escaped with her baby brother. The baby is so terribly skinny. I don't think he will make it. He is all she cares about. He is her only family.

Everyone who meets these two children is affected. One of the nurses had to quietly walk away. She began to cry, and one of the men walked her outside.

The little girl never looked up into anyone's eyes. She seemed very sweet. She just sat there looking out the window, resting her chin on her little brother's head.

She was too weak to cry.

Protection Office

I met a group of eight 13- to 16-year-old boys.

One of the boys, Misago, talked about a rebel attack on February 12, 2001. Many people were killed or severely injured. They were attacked in the middle of the night. In the morning he saw all the dead bodies.

Misago walked with his friend for one week. They were picked up by a military truck.

The soldiers asked them, "Where are your parents?"

"Killed."

He is very soft-spoken.

He heard about the camp through BBC Radio.

Misago's father was killed in June of 2000. His mother was killed six months later in December. They had all been living together in a military camp that was attacked. Misago crossed the border and came here. Now he is a refugee.

He is being interviewed to be registered in this camp, even though he is set to be transferred to another camp tomorrow.

I am so happy this place is here for him. Everyone likes him. In this office he can be a person—not just a number. Here he can try to get the help he needs.

Recruitment camps are set up by the government to try to group people together. You have to stay within the camp so as not to be mistaken for a rebel.

It seems they are all caged—stuck—in the middle of this war.

Misago is also trying to trace his brother.

UNHCR officers started discussing his situation. He was

scheduled to be moved with the other boys to a place (another camp) to build their own home.

These eight boys have only eaten recently because Venice (one of the UNHCR officers) had given them money from his own pocket. The boys have been sleeping on the floor in the offices. They weren't able to get food because they weren't registered yet.

Another young boy came in. He was around fourteen or sixteen years old. He had been traveling on his own, but he met another young boy crossing the border.

He kept looking at me—maybe because I was new, or maybe because I was trying so hard not to let tears fall. My eyes were watery. I don't know how many more stories I can hear.

"Father?"

"Dead."

He had been living with his grandmother. She was too old to run when they were attacked at night.

Both of the boys were dressed in shreds. Their dirty clothes were full of holes and so big they were falling off.

He looked as if he was going to cry at any time.

He was asked, "What do you want from UNHCR?"

He answered, "Help me find my grandmother."

I expected him to say food or shelter—something necessary for himself—but he just wanted her safety. He wanted to see his grandmother.

Another boy walked in when the last left. His hands were at his sides. His eyes were to the floor. He was about fourteen years old.

The UNHCR officers had decided to try to talk to the head of the protection office to keep all the boys in this camp.

Three of the boys think they know in which other refugee camps they can find their relatives. They should stay here if there is a chance they can be reunited with them. It is possible the relatives have not been moved.

These eight boys are children, and they should be placed in a temporary shelter. They don't need a new camp where they have to register all over again.

The officials decided not to interview the rest of the boys. The third boy (who had just walked in) was told it was not necessary to give an interview.

There was something about the way he slowly backed up out of the room, and bowed his head, that made me so sad. It was more than being polite. He was so submissive.

I have a feeling he was recently abused or traumatized—a young boy so defeated, his face so sad.

I pray these boys will be all right. It is scary to realize that they are only eight in over twenty million. What are their chances?

Many of the rest of the day's interviews were cases of registration or follow-ups of recent interviews or needs that had to be addressed.

It's good to know these people have an office to come to where they can have a voice.

There are so many refugees! You can imagine how many things can fall through the cracks.

UNHCR is here to protect the human rights of the refugees—their basic human rights.

Reinstatement

Refugees are interviewed in order to state their case to become a citizen of a new country. They need a safe place to start a life again. Most of the people will live in camps, hoping for peace one day so they can return to their own country.

Without the reinstatement they feel trapped—not even allowed to be a citizen of the place they now live in.

A nineteen-year-old girl came in. Her entire story was too complicated to write. She kept wiping tears away as she spoke. She wants to find her family. After living with them in a refugee camp, she became separated from them and was left behind. She believes her family was resettled in Canada.

A man came in who wanted to be reunited with his wife and children. He was separated from them in one of the camps, and then they were sent to Canada. He has found them, but his ability to join them is a whole other matter.

He took out dusty photos his wife had sent him. They did seem happy in their new home. While pleading for help to be reunited with them, he pointed. . . .

"My wife."

"My son."

"My daughter."

"My baby."

I realize that unless all the right bureaucratic paperwork and processing is done properly, this man will not be able to get back to his family.

As we were driving away to go to our next stop, I saw the young boys I had seen earlier sitting together in the dirt. None of them were talking. They were all just looking out at the road.

I don't know what to do. Somehow I need to do something to help these people. If you could meet them—you would too.

Lunch at the "Sheraton Inn"

I had lunch with Alexandra and a few other field officers. I think it's their joke, "The Kasulu Sheraton Inn." It's a small hut with dirt floors. We had rice and beans . . . again.

I love these field officers here. They talk about the crazy situations but laugh occasionally. If they didn't I think they would go crazy.

The truth is many of the situations they are in are very dangerous.

It is not at all a comfortable or easy life. But they care about these refugees so much they don't want to be anywhere else.

At one point they mentioned "the church" and "the bridge," but then they quickly said, "We can't talk about that." They said they still see the images. "Sometimes you just cry."

Sitting with these men (and Alexandra) I thought of how happy I was to know them—to know they exist. I had wanted to meet good people working in a good organization so I could find a place to start learning and helping. I could not have found a better group.

I later found out what "the church" memory was. I didn't

ask them at the time because I could tell they didn't want to re-member. Now I understand. I asked Alexandra when we got home.

She put her head in her hands, and then she looked at me. She wasn't here when "the church" genocide happened, but the story haunts her.

During a crisis, thousands of people (as many as they could fit inside) hid from the rebels by packing into a church—thinking it would be the only safe place—a house of God.

The rebels found them hiding there and threw in grenades. Then they walked over all the dead bodies, stabbing them to make sure they were dead.

The UNHCR staff members I met this afternoon were among the first people to find them. One woman was found alive. Dead bodies had fallen on her, covering her during the attack.

When they got there they found her rummaging through the bodies.

She was looking for her husband and six children. No one else was alive. If I were her I would have wished to be dead. How do you survive something like that?

We came upon a group of Burundi drummers. Three men and about five children were gathered together. The men are start-ing to teach the next generation. They don't want to lose their culture.

As we drove up closer to them, there was the most won-derful sound—fast, strong, and passionate.

The men and boys took turns in front, drumming and dancing.

I was told what they were chanting.

They wished me a good life!

These refugees are going through so much, and they are wishing me a blessing. They smile and dance and wish me a good life.

My life is so much easier than theirs. It is a strange feeling to receive this blessing, but I accept and I am deeply grateful.

I found out today that a plane is available and that tomorrow I'll be going home.

Friday, March 9

I am in the car. We are about to leave to take a plane to Dar es Salaam. I am very lucky to be on this flight.

We got up at 6:20 A.M. There was no electricity. I am packing my final things with a flashlight. I moved so quickly in the dark. I thought, I am leaving today and I will be gone before I know it.

It is very cold this morning, and I think about how cold it must be for the refugees in the small mud homes—the homes they made.

They have no electricity. They never know how much food will be available on distribution day. The nights can be so cold. They have to make firewood every day.

All the clothes on the children are rags. Some only wear small sheets of red cloth. When funds were cut for sanitary napkins, the red cloth was distributed so the women could at least wrap themselves up during their menstrual cycle, but it was explained to me that the women would go without. How they do it I don't know. The women would rather the children stay warm, or at least warmer.

It is cold and foggy. It took the little plane we were about to board three attempts to land. We waited—our bags on the grass—looking out at the dirt landing.

I was so hungry. I grabbed the last of the bread as we were running out the door. No coffee this morning—no electricity.

We finally took off and arrived just in time to catch the second plane.

I am so tired and hungry but at least I know when I will eat. Very soon I'll have a hot shower and food.

I hope I will never forget how much I have learned. I hope I always appreciate all that I have.

I had no idea what people are going through all over the world. It is worse than I had imagined, and I know I have only begun to see things, I have only begun to understand.

I have been here in Dar es Salaam for a few hours, waiting to make sure I am on a flight to London with a connection to Los Angeles.

I haven't thought or felt anything other than "keep moving."

I am now on a British Airways flight to London.

I realize I am the dirtiest person on the plane.

"Do you want a paper? We also have magazines. Would you like *Vogue* or *Vanity Fair?*"

"No, thank you."

I do say yes to any food they offer me—cashews, pretzels, Coke with lemon. I don't usually eat like this. I feel like a little kid.

They just handed me socks rolled up with a bow around them, an eye mask, a travel kit, and a sleep suit.

Suddenly, the idea of taking off this dirty jacket upsets me. It has been my blanket. I don't want to clean up or wash off this place.

These three weeks have been a new world for me—a special time—I have changed. I like who I became here.

For some reason, taking off my jacket, I feel I am detaching myself from all the people—the places. . . .

The boy on the dirt floor holding his legs.

The eight-year-old girl with her little baby brother in her arms.

The man in the amputee camp who looked into my eyes and told me his story.

The images are like a slide show, flashes of their faces, their bare feet.

I am not sure what I feel. I have never felt so much.

I have to sleep now.

It is both easy and hard to feel guilty leaving.

From this moment on—wherever I am, I will remember where they are.

Mission to Cambodia

From July 16 through July 27, 2001, I undertook a mission on behalf of UNHCR to Cambodia.

Monday, July 16

So here I am again, on my way to Cambodia via Geneva. About an hour ago I left my home.

I was suddenly aware of how safe my home felt. This time I know the things I will see, and I know there is also so much I am unaware of that I am about to discover.

I am embarrassed to realize (and to admit) how much I was able to return to my life after Africa. I know I was able to do so because I kept in touch and have continued to try to help from a distance. But it's easy to make phone calls and send letters and funds from the comfort and safety of your own home.

Maybe I think I should feel guilty for my ability to come and go from these places when others have no choice. I know one thing. I know I appreciate everything more. I am so grateful for my life.

I continue to be indebted to those people around the world. I wanted to help them, and I realize more and more every day how they have helped me.

I am writing by the light of morning just breaking through. Mine is the only window shade up. But only a little. Everyone is asleep on the plane.

I can't sleep. I have five more hours until I reach Zurich, then a few more hours to Geneva.

Hours after I arrive I will be meeting the High Commissioner for Refugees. It will be an honor, as it would be to meet anyone who has dedicated his or her life to helping others. Be it someone who helps millions of people from countries around the world, a great parent to a child, a caring teacher to her class, or just a good friend—all are equally important in this life. When they say, "Each person can make a difference," I believe that is true.

I have many questions to ask the High Commissioner.

How is it that in today's world with all our awareness, abilities, and resources, over 800 million people go to bed hungry every night?

How long have there been refugees from Rwanda? Hundreds of thousands were forced from their homes and not properly given care and shelter.

I will not be asking him for answers. I know UNHCR (United Nations High Commissioner for Refugees) has limited resources. I know all I have stated are his frustrations as well, but maybe he can help me understand how rebels in Sierra Leone can attack so fiercely, cutting off limbs of thousands, and forcing tens of thousands out of their homes.

Why are these rebels not seen as enough of a threat to be removed from power? It seems there are steps being taken, but the process looks as though it could go on for years, leaving many in refugee status.

Many refugees are victims of war—political, religious—and other forms of persecution. In their initial chaos of fleeing and seeking safety in another country, most victims lose virtually every right and material possession that forms the corner-stone of any civilized society—their homes, personal belongings, schooling and health care, close family members and friends, and sometimes even their identities.

As good as the camps can be, they only provide just enough for basic survival to an otherwise doomed people. They are still, in fact, camps.

The walls that protect them also close them in. The borrowed land they are on is often surrounded by local people, who see them as a burden, often unwelcome. In some cases, there is so much violence against them that the refugees are forced to move again. Sometimes they have to go back into the danger of their homeland.

Tuesday, July 17

Geneva

The sky outside my hotel window is clear blue. I just received a fax as I walked into the hotel. It was from Luong Ung. After speaking out about my love for Cambodia and my horror at the land mine situation there, I received a letter from Luong and her book, *First They Killed My Father*. After reading it I was nervous to speak to her. She had become my hero. I got in touch with the Vietnam Veterans of America Foundation (VVAF), where she is the spokesperson for the Campaign for a Landmine Free World. The fax is about a possible visit to the Khien Khleang Rehabilitation Clinic. It also tells me that she will be on the same plane as me from Bangkok to Phnom Penh tomorrow.

She writes, "How exciting to be meeting for the first time at the gate to Thailand."

She told me about Battambang. This was her grandmother and her mother's home province, as well as the birthplace of many uncles, aunts, and cousins. She has not been back there since she was three or four years old.

She also writes about wanting to join me when I visit the Hazardous Areas Life-Support Organization (HALO).

The HALO Trust is a nonpolitical, nonreligious NGO (nongovernmental organization) that specializes in removal of the debris of war.

Over the past eight years forty-three HALO staffers have been killed or maimed, a sacrifice that has saved many thousands of lives. The organization is concerned solely with deactivating mines and not the politically sensitive campaign against their manufacture and deployment.

It is just past 7 P.M. I have spent the last couple of hours at UNHCR headquarters.

I continue to be amazed at the dedication they have to their work.

I was taken to the basement. This is where they all gather together when there are emergencies. It is where they go when they need to solve problems as quickly as possible. So often they are contacted to help a mass of people in just a matter of a few hours.

• • •

Elba was there. Five months ago, she and I met in Sierra
Leone. At that time she showed me photos of her family and
spoke of spending more time with them.

I remember her telling me about one Christmas when she
was suddenly (within seventy-two hours) living in Africa, lay-
ing down plans for structures and programs to help with an
emergency situation.

Now she is in Geneva preparing for her next mission. As
long as there are emergency situations and she knows she has
the ability to help, I don't think she could ever turn her back or
stay at home too long.

You realize everyone here feels this way.

They volunteer to be anywhere in the world to help others. They put themselves in danger of being beaten up, raped,
and maybe even killed (as some have been).

There is a kindness they showed to me and to each
other—a softness and a sadness. They have all been witness to
the worst suffering in this world. They know loss and death,
but they also know the value of friendship and hope. They
have had to rely on each other in their darkest hour.

I met Kofi Annan and found out that he started in
UNHCR. He was very kind.

He had given a speech earlier that day to everyone in the
office. I am sorry I missed it. Everyone was talking about how
good it made them feel. They spoke about his honesty and how
he answered their questions in a straightforward, clear manner.

Someone asked him to talk about the difficult times the
organization is having now. He told them there has been a 20

percent cutback in funds (already receiving only 2 percent of the U.N. funds). And in the last few years, they have begun to assist not only refugees but also internally displaced persons (IDPs).

He didn't promise them he could make it better. He acknowledged their struggle, and he said, "UNHCR has had difficult times before and most likely will again, but through it all, they have always managed to continue to do good."

I had dinner with the High Commissioner, Ruud Lubbers; his executive assistant, Shoko Shimozawa, his chef de cabinet, Yacoub Ali El-Hillo, and the Head of Private Sector and Public Affairs for UNHCR, Pierre-Bernard Le Bas.

It seemed strange at first, but I soon realized that was only because I expected to meet someone who would seem superior or at least very serious. To my surprise, the High Commissioner was very funny—very human. He told us stories of his politics as well as personal stories of his family.

What was most impressive to me was how curious he was of all of us at the table. He was never judging and genuinely valued all of our differences and all of our opinions.

I learned many things—too much to write. What was most interesting was the mix of people he made sure were at the dinner. He told me he did it on purpose.

I was the American. At times during the night I was proud of that and at other times I was not. Everyone seemed to feel the same way about their own country. No one at the table wanted to be right. No one pretended to know the answers. Some of us were more optimistic than others, but all respectfully listened and learned from one another. If that is the essence of this organization—or the essence of what the United Nations is—then I could see tonight how it just might be the answer.

There was a talk tonight about a recent focus on ourselves. People and governments seem to have become more internal. We need to think on an international level. Globally.

I am not sure what day it is.

I took off from Geneva for Zurich this morning. From Zurich I have been traveling over nine hours and I am about to land in Bangkok, where it is 6:05 A.M. Here I will meet UNHCR contacts and hopefully find Luong.

Two hours in Bangkok and then on to Phnom Penh—from there to Siem Reap.

As soon as I was off the plane I met Jahanshah and Marie-Noëlle, two UNHCR field officers. They told me it was Thursday, July 19, which of course means the first few dates recorded in this journal may be confusing. I was recording L.A. time. Cambodia is fourteen hours ahead of Los Angeles.

Also met Ravut, who is a Cambodian ex-refugee now working with UNHCR.

We spoke for two hours and then a man walked up and gave me a note.

Luong Ung is here.

I stepped out of the room to the main lounge area. It only took moments for our eyes to meet. We smiled as we walked up to one another, and we hugged as if we had known each other for years.

Everyone in Cambodia wants to maintain the peace. They

have been through so much. The people of this country are an amazing example of what can be done. Everyone talks of the tremendous courage of the refugees. All of UNHCR have a great respect for these refugees and are very proud to be working with them.

Jahanshah, Marie-Noëlle, and I had lunch at Katie's apartment. She is also with UNHCR and speaks Khmer. It's a beautiful language. Just hearing it made me want to learn it.

Later today we met back up with Luong to travel toward HALO on yet another plane. She said she was "so lucky." I couldn't believe I heard these words from a woman who has had an extremely difficult life, if not the most challenging, horrifying life of anyone I have ever met.

We arrived at HALO Trust in Siem Reap, and we started off on a three-and-a-half-hour journey by road. I feel like I've been traveling for a week.

I pulled out a bag of tapes that a friend packed for me. Katie picked the Beatles 1967 to 1970. Ravut said he liked Santana. We smiled at each other. Around the world—not so different.

In the van they began to talk about amazing musicians they once had in Cambodia. They said of one, "He was like your Elvis, but Pol Pot killed him."

Along the road we passed many small huts with chickens running around outside. On a beautiful day, like today, you smile when you see the little children playing.

There are people carrying water. Long wooden poles are held behind their neck and shoulders. Buckets of water are balanced on each end.

This country almost looks lik[...] intended—God, Allah, Buddha, the G[...]

Then it dawns on you that these [...] they live. It is all they have, and the t[...] jungle that surrounds them has not been [...]

The road we were traveling on led to the Ang Long Veng. Only two years ago this area was where Pol Pot lived and died. His grave is up here. Only as recent as in May '98 were people repatriated here.

HALO Headquarters

It was like an army barracks.

The head of the Ang Long Veng office, Matthew, greets us. He tells us where our quarters are. We are four women. They have four little rooms for us. Ravut, Mao, and twelve other men sleep in the main room lined with cots. They are the best they have and better than I was expecting. Still, it is clear to me, as always, that these humanitarian aid workers do not live far above the living standard of the area. However, unlike the local people, here we have a toilet and a shower.

The lights went out during dinner (white rice and meat). They explained to us how they share power with the hospital and that they might be performing surgery. We were all quiet and sat very still in the dark for a few moments until someone flicked on a lighter. I noticed thunder in the sky. I also heard it on the drive here. I always thought that thunder was impossible with no rain.

ent to my room first. I am exhausted.

I am now in bed writing this under a mosquito net in room number 2.

I have discovered that all the cell phones don't work in this area. I had been planning to call home or at least leave a message that I have arrived here and I am safe.

The HALO officer said I could use the satellite phone tomorrow if it was an emergency. I hope I can find another way. I don't want to have to ask that of them.

The room below the guest quarters looks like a meeting room. On my way to my room I couldn't help but notice all the bomb casings.

When you really look at them you can't help but realize that they are not being made by these local field soldiers (even though they do improvise). These weapons and explosives were originally made by manufacturing plants run by governments like mine.

Friday, July 20

I am writing by a small shaft of light coming in through the wood boards on the wall. I don't know what time it is. About an hour ago I woke up. My feet are itching like crazy. Somehow through the net I was stung a number of times on the bottom of each foot. I am not looking forward to putting my boots on.

I hear sounds of motorcycles, trucks, whistles, and dishes clanging. After a while, the roosters began to crow.

My shower was neither hot nor cold. Just a pump to pour water over you.

For breakfast I had instant coffee and a fish sandwich.

HALO

HALO's goals are to return mined areas of land back to the local community for development. HALO is a UK NGO based out of London. They conduct mine clearance operations and dispose of unexploded shells all over the world. They are nonpolitical, nonreligious. They are neutral. They have great strength in working with the local staff. In Cambodia there are 900 locals working.

Fifty percent of land mine victims die, either at the moment of explosion or from bleeding to death. The 50 percent who survive are nearly all serious amputees.

We drive in HALO Land Rovers to Toul Prasat, where they have cleared a large area. Now there is a school and two wells.

We sit under a blue tarp on two wooden benches. A map lies in the center. Three local Cambodian men working with HALO explain the map: 56,593 square meters need to be cleared; 49,268 square meters have been cleared.

The map shows the green area is cleared. The white area not cleared yet. The red dots are symbols for seventy-two land mines found and forty-plus bombs.

Skull and crossbone symbols represent accidents. There are three.

They point to one, "He lost his leg." Then another, "He lost an eye and his arm."

Blue circles are wells.

A man talked to us about safety. A plastic orange stretcher was behind him as he talked.

Four poles were shown to us.

Red is used for where explosives were found. About ten feet in front of us are four red poles.

Red and white are used for boundaries.

Blue means cleared.

White means not cleared. He then shows us some major trauma kits.

He also gave us a very serious order, "If you hear explosions while you are in the minefield—don't move."

This minefield is one of forty-seven that HALO is now clearing in Cambodia.

We stop at a school next to the minefield.

The school is only for first and second grade. The children are between six and fourteen years old. There are only four teachers for over 240 children.

These teachers have not been paid. If they had been, it would only be about $15 a month.

When the school was built by the government the area had not been cleared for mines. When HALO checked the road the children took to school, they found five explosives just a step from where the kids were walking.

I look around where I am standing. I see so many faces. So beautiful. So many children.

Before HALO they were all living here in minefields out of necessity.

Today two land mines were discovered. I was allowed to detonate one of them with TNT. I must say it was a great feeling to destroy something that would have otherwise hurt or possibly killed another person.

After the explosion, Luong explained how many refugees, herself included, were frightened the first time they were in the United States for the Fourth of July fireworks.

We had white rice, meat, and vegetables for lunch. Then we packed for tonight.

Luong, Matthew, and I will take motorbikes to a small village where we will sleep this evening.

The best way to know the people and the land is to understand what cleared areas can become and to spend time with the local people.

First, we will all go to a resettled area that HALO cleared. UNHCR helped reintegration there.

We stopped by the side of the road where about eight children and two women were using a well that had been built by UNHCR in 2000.

The amazing thing about this whole area is that in only two years, with the hard work of NGOs like HALO, U.N. organizations, and other governments all pitching in to help, as well as the hard work of the local families themselves, the refugees were able to start their lives over.

For many of these people it has been twenty-five years since they have been home.

As we walked around, more people, mostly children, came over to us.

We drove on, then stopped again, this time at Trapeang Prasat.

This was a temple built at the same time as Angkor Wat. Now it is mostly rubble and all overgrown. Still, incense and candles are burning.

Like most Buddhist temples, it was covered in land mines and has just recently been cleared.

In this area, only in the last two years has Buddhism been allowed again—only since the land was taken back from the Khmer Rouge.

During the time of Pol Pot, they outlawed Buddhism and tried to kill all the monks. I am told only about forty survived, hidden by disguises.

Behind the old temple is a newly restored pagoda. On the roof, bright yellow and orange prayer flags fly in the wind.

We take off our shoes and make our way up the boards. I ask if they are sure it is okay. "Yes," I am told, "they welcome visitors."

I remembered that my feet should not face Buddha. I sat on my knees on a mat, my feet facing the other way.

The smell of the incense and the sound of chanting is intoxicating.

Young monks, in traditional orange robes, poke their heads out from a back room. They are very sweet.

The school near here has 1,057 pupils and 27 teachers.

Just recently they were clearing mines next to where these children were playing.

David, a deminer with HALO, points just past where the kids are playing. Only 100 meters down the road is a minefield. Just a fact.

For over an hour on the backs of bikes, Luong and I ride behind two members of HALO.

These roads are closer to the Thai border. They are still very bad.

Cars cannot yet make it across.

It is so beautiful here. I see so much hope. The children do not look malnourished.

I do see amputees along the journey, but they are in makeshift wheelchairs. A man who had lost one leg was riding a bike. His crutch was attached to the front of his bike. He pulled it off to balance himself when he went over a difficult bridge—or what was supposed to be a bridge. Actually, it was just sections of a tree chopped and nailed together.

I know that amputation is a sad fact of life here, but I am so amazed by the pride and strength of these people.

As we continue to ride our bicycles, we pass many men and women watching us from their homes. They are surrounded by their children. They wave or smile at us. Other people just watch us, but I noticed that every time we wave and smile, they immediately respond in kind.

I think some people recognize HALO and know of all the help they have given.

Others are simply curious and want to be friendly to a visitor.

Every time we pass someone on the road, through the jungle and through the little villages, we make eye contact and give a friendly greeting. It is always returned.

Could you imagine if that was our everyday life? Could you imagine acknowledging every individual you pass and smiling at one another? Showing respect to everyone?

We had dinner very early, because we had to go to bed at sundown and get up at sunrise.

A woman took our order, and then we saw a neighbor chase a skinny chicken and catch it. She went into a side room carrying the bird upside down by its legs in one hand and a small butcher knife in the other.

Flies are everywhere.

We cover ourselves in bug spray and simply continue to brush away the flies as we talk.

Drinks are warm and there is no ice.

The floor is dirt. Stray dogs run in and out.

A roll of toilet paper is put on the table. I have become used to that as dinner napkins.

We have been waiting for our food now for about an hour. They had to start from nothing.

It is very hot. We are all dripping in sweat.

There is a mention at the table that "we need to get the hammocks and nets up before it's pitch-black outside."

There are no toilets and no electricity as far as I can tell.

Before we left I was handed a flashlight with extra batteries.

It is dawning on me that I was raised in a city, have never been camping, and I may have a difficult night.

I am excited by the unknown, but we will be on a wooden

pagoda out in the water. What if I have to pee in the middle of the night?

Saturday, July 21

It's morning now. The sun is not up yet but light has broken.

Putting up our hammocks last night was not easy. We used the front lights of our bicycles and stuck three candles between wooden planks.

Luong and I walked to the end of the pier toward land. I had the flashlight. She had two handfuls of toilet paper.

We were smiling in the dark. You could still hear children playing.

We both found spots just off the road about ten feet apart. I turned off the flashlight.

While walking back, lightning struck, illuminating the once black sky. In those sudden moments it was like the light of a full moon. You could see everything, and then it was black again. There was no thunder, just sudden flashes.

Moments later, a heavy rain began. The guys had to help Luong and me move our hammocks to the other side of the boat. The wind was against us. It sounded like the roof was going to come off. The storm happened so suddenly. It was amazing.

It was cold and raining all night. This morning it is still raining. There is talk of the roads and the difficulty.

I began to think of all the people who live here. Their homes do not seem strong enough to still be standing. The rain must have come through the straw roofs, and the dirt floors must now be mud. I had a mosquito net—a luxury they don't have—and still I had bites all over.

We have put on raincoats and are prepared to ride in the rain, but I am told that if the bridges are out we may have to try to get a helicopter.

The rain never stopped. But we continued on, somehow making it through every obstacle.

It seemed every five minutes we had to walk the bikes, either because the bridges were all so broken or because some of the puddles were way too deep. I was leading, so I hit the puddles first. One was so deep the water reached the top of my thighs. At one point, Luong took her shoes off and started looking for frogs.

Once again it began to rain. It was hard for me to see with so much water in my eyes. It isn't easy wearing contact lenses when water is pouring down my face. I think about the fact that if I lived here I wouldn't have the luxury of contacts, and in this weather, with my glasses on I wouldn't be able to see a thing.

We passed more little shacks on the road. There were little children playing with their dogs and chickens. They are smiling. They are amazing.

I saw a woman who was carrying several bundles and beside her was a man on crutches. They both managed to get themselves across the muddy terrain.

Someone asks, "Have you checked for leeches?"

Luong, who was in sandals but is now barefoot, said she had checked and she was okay. Matthew thought he had one on his neck, but he was okay too. The driver told me to make sure I check my feet when I take my boots off.

I have so much respect for these people at HALO. I can't say enough about them. They have even helped to deliver babies who are being born at home. Very few mothers-to-be here ever make it to the local clinic in time.

It is hard to imagine how awful it must have been here during the war. How did they survive all those years of torment and suffering?

After about two hours on the bikes we were picked up by a Land Rover. But that didn't keep us from getting soaking wet. The roads are full of bumps and swerves and tilts. I try to write.

I am cold, tired, and wet, but I have the luxury of knowing that in another hour I will have shelter, towels to dry me off, and food. I am so grateful.

Katie, Mimi, Ravut, and Mao from UNHCR brought me to see a local hospital run by the Médecins Sans Frontières (Doctors Without Borders).

They first came to this province in 1998 (just after Khmer Rouge was defeated) to provide access to health care. They fixed up an old hospital that had been deserted.

They started to work here even before repatriation, working in certain provincial areas.

In 1999, they treated 3,000 malaria patients. Now they have it more under control.

Like HALO and others, these people are also trying to train locals.

It is very important to teach the locals how to help themselves. As other emergency situations come up around the world, and these organizations have to relocate, they do not leave a country unable to continue the programs. In fact, the opposite happens. They always leave the people more self-sufficient.

However, some accidents happen when people try to deactivate the land mines themselves, hoping to use the explosives for fishing.

These doctors have no real surgical facilities, and the medicine is very minimal. They have to take serious cases to other hospitals, but with roads the way they were today (and the rainy season lasts for many months) it becomes impossible to get people there by road.

Due to lack of resources and finance, air travel is very rarely available. Sometimes they mention a Thailand hospital, which may be the only other option, but getting there would be very difficult.

They talk about HIV and how awareness is new here. Many organizations are distributing condoms and trying to give knowledge.

With the new focus on AIDS, the doctors make a point to tell us that so many people with other illnesses still have yet to be dealt with.

The focus will remain on AIDS even though there are still a lot of people to care for in this area who have tuberculosis.

Inside a hospital (which they call a health center), I saw the little room where emergency surgeries take place.

I saw a wooden table with a blue plastic cover.

I was told they don't do blood transfusions.

The last major emergency surgery performed here was the amputation of an arm. The patient was only given basic pain relief.

We walked around the hospital. I met a little girl who looked to be about four years old. She had a patch over her eye.

I saw a little boy who was malnourished. He was brought in because his brother (I think) playfully kicked him out of a hammock. Because he was so terribly malnourished, he hurt his hip. They opened and drained his hip.

The doctors always try to save whatever few anesthetics they have for the children. "If we have—they always receive them first."

All the children here seem so much younger than they are because they are so small. The doctor told me that entire generations are smaller from not enough nourishment. Also, the height of people depends not only on their parents' height, but on the health of the parents and how they were nourished as children.

This is another example of how the war will continue to affect these people for generations to come.

A few hours later, we stopped to meet a returnee family. We just picked a home and asked permission to come in. They were very welcoming.

They laid down a mat for us.

In this little shack lived a mother, father, five children, and a grandmother.

One of the children was deaf and dumb.

Their tiny house was built on stilts to endure the heavily rainy days. To be above the flooding.

The children go to the school that UNHCR built during repatriation.

They have a small plot of land, where they are growing cashew nuts and rice.

The father borrowed a fishing net from a neighbor, but he wasn't able to fish because of all the flooding.

The most amazing feeling I had while sitting with all of them was that it felt like visiting any other family. The difference was that they showed so much more care and affection for each other.

Thankfully, now with peace, their survival concerns are for food and health. They no longer fear the enemy and war causing constant uprooting and running.

During the time we spent with them, aunts, uncles, cousins, and neighbors walked in, crouching in the corners or pressing against the walls.

Everyone was polite. When you catch the eyes of any of them, they smile at you, if only with their eyes.

Sometimes before a question was asked, the person stepped forward and sat in the center, then asked their question.

We met up with Scott from Carere (Cambodia Area Rehabilitation and Regeneration Project) to see a school they had built and to meet the community and to understand the process.

The children were off today. About twenty members of the community all met in a classroom. They spoke about the school's development and needs.

The community is very involved in all stages of development. They are now looking to increase the number of classrooms so more children will be able to attend school.

During the meeting, a coconut with a straw was placed in front of each of us.

They all thanked us for coming and wished us good health.

I feel very fortunate that because of where I live and the job I have, I can help with the schools.

The imbalance of funding in the world makes no sense to me.

The school director tells me that this school serves two villages totaling 1,290 people. There are 590 children between six and ten years old, but there is only room for 370 students. Two hundred and twenty children are not able to go because there just isn't enough room. In each class there are fifty students and there are only three classrooms. Attendance has to be broken up into different times of the day.

Out of the 370 enrolled students only 101 are girls. We are told that with the school so overcrowded, most families keep their girls home to work. Their first priority is to educate their boys.

The school has many more needs. It has no latrines and only one well.

The well is very old and they worry about it not being safe for the children.

Sunday, July 22

I just woke up to roosters. It seems the rain has finally stopped. I hope so, because we have a three-hour boat ride to Battambang this morning. But if it rains, it rains.

It is amazing being around these people from HALO and UNHCR. They put up with so much to try to do their jobs, and yet they always talk about the strength of the people here and all that they have to endure to survive. These workers are here to help the refugees overcome such tremendous odds, and when it happens, it must feel so rewarding.

Scott, who I met yesterday, has been here twenty years. He works with Carere. He is married now to a Cambodian woman who works with the government on women's issues. They have three children.

Scott is working here to ensure education. He is going to help me find ways to fund a few needed school buildings. He said he has the greatest job in the world.

Not only do these aid workers never complain about the difficulties, but they also say they feel very lucky to be able to help.

I must have ten spider bites on the bottoms of my feet. At least I think this is what happened, since the swelling on my feet has gotten bigger. They aren't mosquito bites, but I am still constantly itching. I also have developed a rash on my leg I cannot positively identify.

The food has been strange. I never have a feeling of being full.

Sometimes parts of the day go on for so long, and when we finally get food, it isn't very much.

I also haven't been sleeping very well. It's probably because I am always getting so wet from the rain.

And yet with all of these complaints I have never felt so good in my life. I am so tremendously honored to be with these people. I realize more every day how fortunate I have been in my life.

I hope I never forget and never complain again about anything. But damn—my feet are itchy.

The Boat Ride to Battambang

We drive up a dirt road through the fishing villages.

These people live in such poor conditions, and yet they have such a beautiful spirit. Everyone is working, and their children all seem so happy.

Some families live on small houseboats; others live in small huts on stilts (for when the water rises).

During our boat journey, we pass through villages and see many fishermen.

At one point, the boat started speeding. I was sitting on top. The men in front of me told me where to hold on.

I continue to grow more and more in love with everyone here. They know something—something we have forgotten. It is a feeling of community. It is a feeling of deeply appreciating their peace and freedom.

Off the boat, three hours later, sunburnt and windswept,

we finally arrived. Mao meets us at the boat with the Land Rover. He had left a day before to arrive in time. We stopped for lunch.

After we ordered, the cook told us he had to quickly run to the market because he was out of vegetables. He left us alone and rode off on a bicycle to a nearby market. I don't know why I thought that was so great, but it just was.

During lunch I asked Katie how long it took her to learn to speak Khmer (the Cambodian language). She said that she had only lived here a few years but she had listened and she briefly had a teacher. Mostly, she had made a great effort. Katie spoke of how important it is to be able to communicate with the people. When you speak their language, you will have a better chance of understanding exactly what they need from us—not just assume.

How could we ever pretend to know what is best for a people if we have no clear relationship with them?

Battambang

We visit Emergency, an Italian NGO.

This hospital is used for civilian war casualties and the treatment and rehabilitation of land mine victims.

They also have a school for children.

They had two in Afghanistan, but one was already closed by the Taliban.

In the children's classroom they have pictures on the walls that they all drew. The drawings are of flowers, butterflies, and two self-portraits of kids in wheelchairs.

Marco was the name of the Emergency doctor who was showing me around the hospital.

They have (and always need) a stock of blood. The room is cold. The blood is kept in the refrigerator.

"Are you squeamish?" he asked me. No.

He took me into Intensive Care.

All I want to say is thank God this hospital and these doctors are here.

I met several land mine victims.

One man was gardening with a hoe and a land mine exploded in his face. He lost an eye and he has slight brain damage. For the past two months they have been fixing his jaw. He is so happy to be able to eat normally and talk again.

Another man looked like he was sleeping, but they explained that he was in a coma. He has a bullet in his head.

One of the local staff, a pregnant woman, was shot and killed. Her husband also worked in the hospital. He was the first to see her when she was brought in. She later died of blood loss.

There are so many amputees here.

A man from a land mine advisory group is here looking into a revision of amputations. Young amputees have to be checked regularly. Because these children keep growing, complications continue to occur.

Later on, they took me to the women and children's ward.

One little boy was riding with his father in a cart when they ran over an antitank mine. His father was killed. He came here with many serious fractures and severe blood loss. Emergency found his mother and hired her as a nurse.

I met a man named Buu Chorm. We showed each other our tattoos and shared their meaning. His are for good fortune and protection.

Because he had lost one leg, he joked, saying, "Maybe I should have had more tattoos."

I asked a few doctors what is it they need most. I continued to hear the same answer. They need new roads to the hospital. There are many organizations that are trying to help, but it costs more than a million dollars a kilometer to lay a two-lane asphalt road.

Earlier this morning I was complaining about my feet itching. This afternoon I met a man who lost his leg. He greeted me with a smile and was joking with his doctor. He found the energy to be a gracious host to us visitors.

Samlot

We drive to the UNHCR office, where we will stay for the next few weeks. UNHCR was so helpful here during repatriation, but now that these people are no longer refugees there is no main office here. We are using a room at Action Nor Sud (ANS).

He helped us to a room with three fold-out beds. Mosquito nets were set up by nailing them to the walls.

The small bathroom had a large pot with a small tin bowl in it—for an "elephant bath."

Monday, July 23

It is about 7 A.M. We woke up to roosters and a very hot sun. As I write this, Mimi and Ravut are picking fruit from a tree. They have to jump up to get it.

We head out to visit Samlot Emergency health center first thing in the morning.

This center was built in 1999. War in this area had just ended.

There were hundreds of mines in this area in 1999. Many people died because of them.

Ten more health centers were built in 2001.

They still don't have enough supplies to take care of a big emergency. They have to try to get the victims out to Battambang, but the roads are almost impossible to drive. Sometimes the roads go out.

Every month about 1,500 people in Samlot come in to the health center with malaria.

The head of the Emergency staff told me, "We can only give them so much—sometimes only our hearts."

I visited a malaria ward and a tuberculosis ward.

During the conflict people were not getting polio vaccinations.

Finally, vaccines have become available, and children have been coming to the health center to receive them.

We are driving to our next meeting. This is the first time I noticed the signs along the road. They say, DANGER—MINES, with a skull and crossbones.

So much of the land has still not been cleared.

We are warned, "Always stay on the tracks or follow someone's footpath. It is not a good idea to be wandering around even if there are no signs up."

Every twenty-two minutes, somewhere in the world, a person is killed or maimed by a land mine.

We visit an animation center.

Here they focus on children who have gone through war and conflict.

They emphasize the importance of playtime. They not only focus on beginning education skills for little ones but also on sports and dance.

We spent time with the children. Mao and Ravut played soccer. Katie and I built a house with pieces of wood. We raced with another little boy who was building his own house. We lost.

Some of the children have light hair—a sign of malnutrition.

One little boy with a clubbed foot was playing with an old soccer ball.

The only toys I saw were pieces of wood and two old soccer balls, and yet they all seem so very grateful to have them to play with.

Some children were wearing UNHCR backpacks that were distributed over a year ago. I think they play with them on because they always want to keep their things with them. They probably fear losing all they have again.

As I am writing this I am surrounded by about fifteen little kids. They are curiously watching me write. They are all smiling and giggling. Are they looking at my light skin color, my tattoos, my clean white T-shirt, my light eyes? Maybe they are staring and smiling at me because I am left-handed? In the end, I think they are just being playful with me because I am a new visitor and they are normal, curious children.

We drove into another village and I met locals from the Samlot government health service. They were trained by Emergency to give vaccinations.

For lunch we had rice, meat, and strange-looking fruit with red-and-green stems.

Mimi is feeling sick. I fell asleep for a few minutes and I don't feel so well myself. Anytime someone is sick here people go through a list of questions about symptoms; I guess checking for malaria or anything else that might be serious.

As for me, I think I am just tired. I am not used to such long working days, which of course makes me respect all of these people that much more.

We met up with Sarath, the director of Cambodian Vision in Development (CVD). They provide aid to the most vulnerable returned refugees and internally displaced persons. They are working to help these people help themselves.

While with CVD, I saw a blind man with only one arm. He was gardening. He motioned to his home. Another man walked up and helped to guide him. This man had both of his arms missing, but he could see. The two men were working together. The disabled and other "vulnerables" compensate for their needs by helping each other.

The man with no arms had six children depending on him to provide for them. He speaks of how little rice he is able to plant. His face is so sweet. When he reentered this land after being a refugee—for over eight years in Thailand—he tried to start over, to build a place for his family. As he was clearing a plot of land, a land mine exploded.

His son, a very little boy with big brown eyes, holds on to his father's shoulders. His father leans in and smiles. Only three of his children can go to school now. He can't afford to send them all. It costs 1,500 *riels* per month per child, which is the equivalent of thirty cents in American money.

As he continues to speak, I continue to write. I have started to focus on my notebook because I am very close to crying. I don't want him to feel I pity him or to feel embarrassed by his situation or condition.

He smiles at me and says good-bye. He speaks. It is translated for me. "I don't speak so clearly now. Worry makes your mind weak."

At our second stop, a man with no legs is out in front working in the field. He takes his hat off and greets us with a smile. He uses an oxcart to get to work. I ask if he has children. He points to the missing lower part of his body. He was cut in half, literally. He smiles as if to say, "It's all right. Don't feel bad for asking."

We walked further into the field. We met a blind man whose arms were cut off just past his elbows. He uses his feet to try to clear the land. His wife has mental problems as well, and when she left him, she took the baby. She left him with five other children. Volunteers have to help him cook for his family. He uses his mouth to fish whenever he can. The will of these people to survive is amazing to me.

This man also has a small child with him. The boy looks about five years old, but we are told he is nine. He can't go to school. He is his father's eyes. In this area alone there are 800 cases very similar to this man, most all are land mine victims. I feel so much hate for anyone (a person or a government) who is trying to stop the ban on land mines.

We get back in the car to move on to the next area. Ravut asks if the area they are clearing in their backyards has been demined yet. They answer no, but they are considered safe because none have exploded there yet.

Most people will read that and say, "Why can't they demine it? And if they can't, why are they living there?" They have no choice.

The war was everywhere and every single area could not be demined in time. There were not enough funds and not enough time.

More important, this must not happen again. The use and manufacturing of land mines should be banned. I hope when people read this they will want to help.

I was told of another vulnerable case—a man with no legs who had two daughters. We could not visit them because the roads were so bad from the rain. And the rainy season has just begun. These people have to pray that no emergency happens. They would have no way to get help.

Someone asked one of the men in our car, "Were you a refugee?" He smiled, "Yes." In this group he knows he can be proud and is respected. He told us he was in a camp from 1989 to 1992. He was in a camp in Thailand—Site 2.

Ravut said he was also in Site 2. So was Mao. About 120,000 people were there.

Site 2 was the name given to this refugee camp by the U.N. border relief organization. This refugee camp had the largest population of Cambodian people outside Phnom Penh. People took refuge in these camps during the reign of Pol Pot and the Khmer Rouge. The camp covered less than four square miles, and an estimated 220,000 Cambodians resided there. Site 2 was the most severely crowded camp in all of Thailand.

6 P.M.

We visit night-school classes in the area.

Action Nord Sud provides literacy classes for adults in the early evening. We visited one. We are guided by Anne, a French woman. She runs this NGO. ANS funds 26 teachers in more than 10 schools.

United Nations Educational, Scientific and Cultural Organization (UNESCO) did a survey and developed a curriculum.

United Nations Children's Fund (UNICEF) has helped with training and making and distributing manuals.

Anne said the teachers are mostly women. The classes are at night. Mothers take their children to class. The children all hover around them.

Tonight they are being taught to read, and what they are reading is also information that will help them. They repeat after the teacher in their own language. Even after going through so much they are still a culture.

It is explained to me that they are learning about natural medicine and how it is better than chemical medicine.

Dinner

We had rice, meat, and bananas.

The men spoke a little about their "Pol Pot time" during 1975 to 1979.

While living in the camps they learned English and studied grammar. They were even able to explain to me the difference between "How much?" and "How many?" I was never very good at grammar. How perfect they would be as my teachers.

Ravut shared the story of meeting his wife. They were married in a camp. She is working now for the American Embassy. They have two children—ten and five years old.

I suddenly noticed the sky. The stars here are so clear and bright. The moon is a crescent but not straight up and down. It is almost on its back.

Tuesday, July 24

It is 7 A.M. now. We have all been up for a while. There is something amazing about getting up first thing in the morning to witness a new day begin.

We have just had breakfast. I was very hungry. We had Nescafé, rice, and dried meat and fish. It tasted like oily beef and fish jerky.

I write that not because I am ungrateful, but because I think it says something about these amazing field officers. They are living in these areas for months at a time. They live without so many comforts of home—one of those being a strong shower.

I took another "elephant bath" this morning. I still can't manage to pour the water over myself right and I don't want to waste the water. Yesterday I was about to throw ice out of my glass and Ravut stopped me. "Ice is very expensive here. You should give it back to the kitchen."

The first thing we did today was visit a school.

When refugees were repatriated there were no teachers or schools. For many years these people got very little or no education.

They began training teachers immediately so they could start educating as soon as possible.

ACTION NORD SUD and UNHCR had to press the government to recognize these teachers-in-training as certified teachers. These men and women have much less education than teachers in other areas, but they have been recognized and they will start to be paid. A very low salary but it's something.

In this school the children are six or seven years old. Children are the same all around the world. Beautiful.

It's wonderful to see them learning here—especially their own language and their own culture.

One of the teachers we saw today, with a classroom full of kids, we also saw last night teaching adults.

A teacher shouted something in Khmer and all the children in the three rooms ran out smiling and giggling.

They all line up. They are about to start morning exercises.

Ravut, Mimi, Mao, Ann from ANS, and Sarath from CVD and myself all line up beside the children.

As the exercises start, the children are very organized and disciplined.

We are all over the place—turning the wrong way and swinging our arms into each other.

Most of the kids laugh at us. Some children are shy and watch us with curious eyes. Their heads are down—hiding smiles maybe. I can't tell.

Their eyes looked happy.

It was beautiful to see them so happy. Most photos of these children in the past years have been so sad and awful. We always see them crying and hungry with very little hope in their eyes.

This morning I played with these kids surrounded by lush green trees and a beautiful blue sky, in a school built and run by people who care so much about them. It feels like heaven.

A little boy's hair blows in the wind. He looks up squinting. The sun is in his eyes. He catches my eyes and hides behind a friend. He peeks out. I can't stop smiling.

We now have to make circles. The children start to sing. I can't understand what they are saying, but it sounds so sweet.

Later, it is explained to me that they were singing, "The land is beautiful. Take care of it. It is good to us. But it is not safe. Be careful of dangerous land mines. If we see one, don't touch it."

We went to another area where music was playing. It was an outdoor dance class.

The children were all wearing flip-flops. Some pairs were only about three inches long.

After we had played with them for a little while, the children began to stand closer to us. They seemed less shy. They even seemed to feel safe.

At the second school, children are sitting in the classrooms. You can hear them as we drive up repeating after their teacher. We notice a teacher who is an amputee. He has only one leg and walks with a crutch as he writes on the chalkboard.

I am told twenty-nine of sixty-nine of the teachers are disabled. Everyone is so happy though to have school after all they have been through.

Someone tells me that in Samlot there are about 100 land mines left.

Another teacher walks up to us slowly. She is smiling. She hands Ann a paper. I notice one foot is in a sandal. Her other foot is wooden. There are so many amputee cases and so many land mine victims it starts to feel normal. It is just a common fact of life here.

The paper was a request for a small room of books. There are so few manuals and no libraries.

In one room they are using cut-up bundles of plants to learn to count.

Following the genocide in Rwanda in 1994, an estimated 250,000 Rwandans swept into Tanzania over a period of twenty-four hours. UNHCR/ P. MOUMTZIS

Making friends and sharing secrets with a Sierra Leonean returnee from Guinea at FAWE Girls' Centre in Grafton. UNHCR/ L. TAYLOR

Crafts workshop with young refugee women, among the thousands of victims of persecution, violence, and war in Sierra Leone. UNHCR/ L. TAYLOR

Returnee children in Waterloo Transit Centre near Freetown.
UNHCR/ L. TAYLOR

Sierra Leonean children who were refugees in Guinea. After arriving from
Guinea, they overnight at Jui Transit Centre before continuing their
journey home. Meals are served at the centre. UNHCR/ L. TAYLOR

Amputee victims. Many civilians were amputated in the civil war in Sierra Leone. UNHCR/ L. TAYLOR

Meals are served to Sierra Leonean returnees from Guinea at Jui Transit Centre near Freetown. UNHCR/ L. TAYLOR

The *Fanta* ship carrying Sierra Leonean returnees from Guinea having just arrived at Freetown. UNHCR/ L. TAYLOR

Overnight accommodation facilities for returnees at Jui Transit Centre near Freetown. UNHCR/ L. TAYLOR

Sierra Leonean returnees from Guinea overnight at Waterloo Transit Centre near Freetown. UNHCR/ L. TAYLOR

Sierra Leonean returnees from Guinea who have just got off the *Fanta* ship are waiting to be registered at the port of Freetown. UNHCR/ L. TAYLOR

Children studying at a school UNHCR built for returnees in Samlot.
UNHCR/ M. N. LITTLE

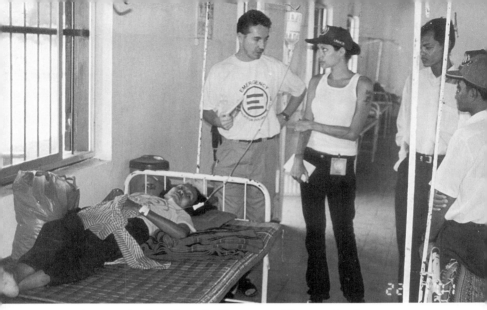

Learning about medical needs at the Emergency Clinic in Samlot. UNHCR/ M. N. LITTLE

Being briefed by staff of an NGO, the Halo Trust, on mine clearance in An Long Veng District. Over 110 million active mines are in sixty-eight countries. UNHCR/ M. N. LITTLE

Women and children are collecting water from a well funded by UNHCR
in An Long Veng. UNHCR/ M. N. LITTLE

A mother with children at the Emergency Clinic in Samlot. The boy is
treated for malaria. UNHCR/ M. N. LITTLE

A girl studying at a school UNHCR built for returnees in Samlot.
UNHCR/ M. N. LITTLE

Pupils exercising outside a school UNHCR built for returnees in Samlot.
UNHCR/ M. N. LITTLE

At a school for Afghan refugee children in Loralai. UNHCR/ S. HOPPER

Watching as Afghan refugees demonstrate how to use the water pump in Zar Karaz II camp in Loralai, Pakistan. UNHCR/ S. HOPPER

Hearing concerns of newly arrived Afghan refugees in Jalozai, Pakistan. In August 2001, Pakistan was hosting over 2 million refugees; many have now returned to Afghanistan. UNHCR/ S. HOPPER

With UNHCR staff visiting an Afghan refugee site in Peshawar, Pakistan.
UNHCR/ S. HOPPER

Talking to participants of the child-to-child teaching program at Nasir Bagh camp for Afghan refugees in Pakistan. UNHCR/ S. HOPPER

Visiting Saranan refugee village in Pakistan. UNHCR/ S. HOPPER

Visiting a school for Afghan refugee children run by Save the Children outside of Quetta, Pakistan. UNHCR/ S. HOPPER

Visiting an Afghan refugee village outside of Quetta, Pakistan. UNHCR/ S. HOPPER

Talking to refugees and UNHCR staff at the Jamaluddin Vocational Centre in Peshawar, Pakistan. UNHCR/ S. HOPPER/ 08.2001

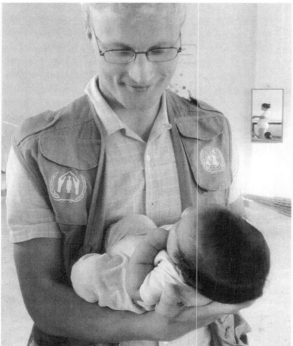

A UNHCR staff member holding a Colombian refugee baby in the shelter for the refugee family. UNHCR/ L. BOSCARDI

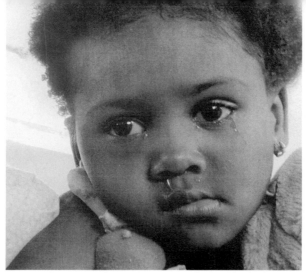

A Colombian refugee child in Ecuador. The long-standing armed conflict in Colombia has left hundreds of thousands dead and displaced more than 1.5 million people. Thousands have fled to neighboring Venezuela, Panama, and Ecuador. UNHCR/ L. BOSCARDI

A Colombian refugee working at a carpentry workshop in Ecuador supported by UNHCR. UNHCR/ L. BOSCARDI

Returning home to Cambodia, April 2003. HOLLY GOLINE

I watch as one of the teachers walks back to his classroom. It seems his prosthetic leg is giving him discomfort. Can you imagine standing and teaching all day, and sometimes also at night, while walking around on a prosthetic leg?

I am hot and uncomfortable and I have only been out a few hours.

These teachers walk miles to get to the school. The roads are very bad.

There is also very limited health care. It is especially difficult and expensive to get a new limb. They also must be changed every few years. Even if they are badly fitted and crudely carved out of wood, they are still a luxury.

In other areas, like Phnom Penh, the services are better, but it is never easy or fair to have a life like this. These people have been suffering for so long.

We drive about eight hours back to Battambang.

Battambang, Tuesday Night

Mimi and I met Bishop Enrique Figaredo S.J. (a Jesuit priest). Everyone calls him Father Kike (pronounced Quique). He is the Bishop of Battambang.

He was in the camps in 1984, helping Cambodian refugees in Thailand. He came to Cambodia in 1988.

He works mostly with land mine victims, but he also helps with polio victims.

He is very kind and charming.

Father Kike is wearing a blue-checkered short-sleeve shirt

with a peace dove sewn on his pocket. He pointed proudly to the little dove.

"Little girl sewed this on for me."

His function in the camps was to help organize programs for the disabled. He kept teaching them skills for when they would go back, but he jokes how years kept passing. Finally, ten years later they have four or five skills.

We all met in a little restaurant. They served ice cream. It was very exciting. Father Kike and I both had chocolate chip ice cream.

Very soon he is going to Nicaragua to be part of a meeting of those who signed the treaty to ban land mines.

He mentions how I could go to Emergency and see what is happening. Every day they care for land mine victims. He said, "Good things happen in the middle of terrible places."

He told me about a little girl who lost her leg while helping her father farm.

When Father Kike spoke of this girl (in his Spanish accent), he said, "Is so terrible, is to cry."

Father Kike, Mimi, and I talk about his learning he had become a bishop. He said, "I got a call from Rome and I thought maybe I got in trouble or something."

He said, "I believe life is not just inside the Church. God is in everything, everywhere."

He admits, "I like dancing—a lot. I bring traditional Cambodian dancing into Church."

Father Kike is a wonderful priest. He is very modest when asked about his life.

He mentions a man we should meet. "He cannot speak English, but you can see what he is doing. You see his family, his life. He feels with his heart; that is best. Do everything with your heart."

He doesn't push his religion. He believes the people of Cambodia have a beautiful faith.

In 1984, another archbishop was killed. Father Kike was afraid when he was appointed. He thought he would surely be killed.

Father Kike speaks of a literacy teacher who has no arms below his elbows. He crosses and connects his upper arm limbs and writes with chalk.

Father Kike smiles proudly at this man and says, "Amazing. The people are so very gentle here. It is so easy to love them."

I can also see how all the people here love Father Kike. They also know they don't have to be Catholics to come to his church for assistance.

Mimi and I are in a hotel tonight. We head back to our rooms.

Signs in the Hotel:

NO GUNS

NO DURIAN

(A strong cheesy-smelling fruit.)

We went to a market earlier today to buy durian.

Mao, Ravut, Marie-Noëlle, and I sat on little plastic stools as we ate it. Mao tried it, and like most Cambodians, he loved it. He said it was creamy. I wondered how he could tell if it was ripe.

Tonight, back in the hotel, as we walked up the stairs to our rooms, the hallway smelled of durian. Someone had snuck some in. We started laughing.

Wednesday, July 25—7 A.M.

No phone in the hotel, but the cell phones are working. We are finally getting a signal.

We had some Quick Coffee. All the milk is condensed like sweet syrup.

I think I'm beginning to like it.

We left for the airport for an 8:30 plane to Phnom Penh.

Our first meeting there was with Scott and Joanne with Carere.

They had put together a program for the building of new schools.

I then met with the Minister of Education and the Deputy Prime Minister. He's grateful to the U.N. and all NGOs, but they stress the importance of everyone working together. He believes the focus must be on equal education opportunities for rich and poor, girls and boys.

So much needs to be done. They will need as much help as they can get from the international community.

We visited the Veterans International Rehabilitation Centre, open since 1991.

Vietnam Veterans of America Foundation is where Luong is the spokesperson for the Campaign for a Landmine Free World. She met us at the door and introduced us to Larry. He is American but lives here and runs this center. He has two beautiful adopted Cambodian children; a girl and a younger boy who sat in on our meeting.

Facts

The U.S. State Department estimates that there are 60 to 70 million land mines in the ground worldwide and a third of the world's nations are mined.

To harm civilians, combatants often place land mines on the side of roads, near schools, and in agricultural fields.

The goal of the rehabilitation center:

"TO GIVE TO THOSE WHO SURVIVE THE WAR—A CHANCE TO SURVIVE THE PEACE"

Kent Wiedemann, the U.S. Ambassador for Cambodia, joined us this afternoon at the rehabilitation clinic. He told me that the U.S. military is now being trained to help victims of trauma.

Teams of six or seven doctors and nurses are here visiting to learn. They speak in abbreviated terms:

BK means below the knee.

AK means above the knee.

It is easier to make a BK prosthesis.

Larry says, "My son is a BK." I then realize the little boy is wearing two sneakers with one foot made of wood.

There is a small factory at the center of the clinic that manufactures and fits prosthesis limbs. BKs cost $150, and AKs cost about $200.

Hand hooks and wooden hands are given to arm amputees.

I saw men with recently fitted legs practicing kicking a soccer ball back and forth.

A three-year-old lost her leg from infection. As long as her bones keep growing, she will have to be checked on a regular basis to have her prosthesis leg replaced to fit her new growth.

I met two blind land mine victims who work at the center helping to build the prosthesis limbs and also putting the spokes on wheels for wheelchairs.

The wheelchairs are given out free of charge.

There are also baby walkers for small amputees.

World Food Program (WFP) helps by giving food. They have an outreach program in the field every day.

They always need roads repaired and ramps built.

The U.S. spends three million dollars a year to fund demining groups like HALO, MAG (Mines Advisory Group), and CMAC (Cambodian Mine Action Center). They spend one million a year on rehabilitation projects.

Cambodia is one of the ten poorest countries in the world. In Asia, it has the highest infant mortality death from AIDS.

I believe the U.S. ambassador cares deeply for all the people here. He desperately wants to continue to help eliminate poverty.

Later that afternoon, Ravut, Mao, Mimi, and I visited Tuul Sleng, the Genocide Museum. In the past it was a school. Pol Pot transformed it into a prison and called it "5-21." It is the former Khmer Rouge 5-21 Prison.

Several thousand victims were here.

I saw a picture of Pol Pot (next to a picture of monks in front of a wall of skulls).

The picture of Pol Pot was black and white. I could see he was giving orders—and knowing what those type of orders were, the image made me sick.

A monk walks beside us.

I was shown graves of fourteen people who were killed just before the Khmer Rouge left. Only a few hours later and they might have survived.

The cells are open to walk through. They have not been changed. In each one of the cells there is a picture of the person who was tortured. The picture is exactly of the room when the soldiers found them. What it looked like the day it was discovered. Throughout the prison there are so many pictures to see and records available to read. It is horrible what happened here.

As I continue to write this I think, What am I doing? How can I be standing here? I can't breathe. I want to stop writing. I don't believe in ghosts but—I can't describe the pictures and the cells. I don't know what to say.

Suddenly, amidst all this horror, I smell incense. I am told the monks are praying.

We continue to walk through the cells. I saw how people were chained to their beds. The clamps are still on the old metal frames. I asked, "How did they go to the bathroom?" I was told, "Just there on themselves."

I know what this feeling is now—I realize it is fear. I am scared here.

I enter another room filled with ID photos that were taken away from the people before they were tortured and killed. Ravut said, "I don't want to see too much more. I am afraid to see my father's picture. I am not sure which place they took him to to kill him, but I have a feeling it was very near here."

All the faces in these photographs are scared and very tired. I saw some pictures taken from the sides of their faces. I asked, "What is that attached to their head?" Ravut tells me, "It is a drill. They would slowly drill into your head until they killed you."

There are so many faces of young and old men and women and so many children, even babies.

There are pictures of the instruments and the ways people were tortured, and there are walls of pictures of the dead after being killed by these devices. It is very clear in each picture exactly how they died.

I am told fifteen minutes from here are "the Killing Fields."

There is a half statue of Pol Pot with a black X. The black X is sprayed over a Cambodian word. Ravut told me it means "bravo"; obviously a statue Pol Pot had made for himself.

Barbed wire covers the prison's balcony, intended to prevent desperate people from committing suicide.

The cells have brick-and-cement walls. They were built to break up a once larger room into three-by-seven foot cells. They are all dusty and crude. Blood stains still cover all the walls.

I keep thinking about how I want to get out of here.

I was taken to another room that had many pictures of Pol Pot, his family, and his troops. I won't look at him. I walked away.

Ravut showed me on maps where Pol Pot started his genocide and where he moved to from year to year.

I was shown a photo of the man who was the famous Cambodian singer, who Ravut said was like our Elvis, but Pol Pot had him killed.

There is a display case full of signs describing the pictures of the instruments of torture. We all stood in front of it, in silence, for what seemed to be a very long time.

I saw photos of babies being ripped away from their mothers. I saw photos of mothers being killed as they held their babies in their laps. In one photo a mother still had the drill in her head and her baby in her lap.

On one wall there is a map of Cambodia made out of human skulls. I read pages and pages of destruction.

There was a picture on the wall of babies being thrown up

in the air and then caught by being stabbed and killed with the blade of a bayonet.

I saw pictures of men holding babies upside down by their legs and squashing their little heads against a tree.

I have to get out of here. I have to step outside. I can't breathe.

Wednesday Night

Marie-Noëlle and I had mentioned to Ravut and Mao that we would love to meet their families. We had heard so much about them. Tonight we were invited to dinner at Ravut's home. He has a beautiful family—a lovely wife and two girls ages six and eleven. Mao is also with us. He came with his sweet wife and their three children, ages three, one and a half, and an adorable seven-month-old baby boy.

I am honored to know these people. I hope that one day, after many visits, we will become closer friends. I do feel I can say we already are friends, sharing and laughing.

Ravut has many books in his house: law, history, a French and English dictionary, etc. Many of these he studied while he was a refugee in the camps. The women also work. It seems everyone at the table works with an NGO or a government office. They are all amazing women and they are much more knowledgeable about many things than I am. I wonder what they would have been able to do with the education and opportunities I was offered. They wouldn't have wasted a moment.

They explained how expensive air-conditioning is so we use fans. The lights went out for a short while so we used candles.

It was a beautiful evening.

We were all very quiet at first, but it didn't take us long before we were falling off our chairs laughing.

The kids were so happy, all playing together. I felt so grateful to be able to be there.

Thursday, July 26

So many nightmares last night. Hardly slept.

We visited the Jesuit Refugee Service (JRS) today.

When we stepped out of the car we were greeted by a young girl with only one leg named Song Kosal. She handed me a package with a wooden bird of peace key chain.

She lost her leg when she was five years old. She was looking for firewood with her mother.

Tun Channareth also greeted us with a big smile. He is in a wheelchair. His friend, who is almost always with him, has a crutch. He has one leg. They joke, "We get around with one leg between us."

Most handicapped people work with others who are handicapped. It gives inspiration. The priests and nuns at JRS do everything they can, from taking kids to the hospital to making the mosquito nets. They also analyze the data to evaluate the overall progress of the Landmine Ban Treaty.

There are many beautiful pictures on the walls here—

pictures depicting humanity, compassion, and prayerful meditation.

Most of the volunteers here are nonreligious. Everyone who works here at the Jesuit Relief Service is kind, warm, and very humble.

We drove to Banteay Prieb Rehabilitation Centre, one of the JRS's main areas of work.

We visit the Centre of the Dove, a learning place for men and women disabled by land mines, war, and polio. It used to be an army communication center.

There are many workshops here. They make eighty wheelchairs per month. A man with no legs is on the table making parts. The need for wheelchairs is so great. They can't ever seem to make enough.

The next workshop is a sewing school. I met two women with big wooden looms working hard at making scarves. Two other women are busy at their sewing machines making backs for wheelchairs.

A Spanish priest joined us and told us jokes and a story about one of the students here being a terrible math student. He thought an average-size window was 125 meters wide. Now he is one of the best social workers here. He is often the one who rushes to the hospital, driving new victims of land mines.

There are seventeen students in the wood sculpture class. They are making so many beautiful pieces. They are learning a trade so in the future they can make a living.

One student is making a wooden chalice for Bishop Kike to hold the Holy Communion wafers.

Next to her, a few other sweet men and women are making

wooden Buddha statues. Their tools are very basic for sculpturing, yet their workmanship is amazing. There are handicap ramps leading to all the buildings here.

Other workshops include an electronics class, an agriculture class, and a welding class in which people learn to make hospital-bed frames. There are also classes in which one can learn regular education—the basics like reading and writing and math.

The Centre of the Dove is truly an amazing place. I don't know what all these people would do without it. All the programs are focused on giving handicapped people a real future. I have just learned that this land belongs to the government and the Centre of the Dove has been given a set time to be here. Next year the government can demand a lot of money and these programs will start to suffer.

Dinner with UNHCR Staff

During this trip I was asked to be the Goodwill Ambassador for UNHCR. I can't express how happy and honored I was. The UNHCR field officers then told me, "We are so happy to be the first to congratulate you on your appointment as Goodwill Ambassador to UNHCR. Remember, we are in 120 countries. You have family wherever you go." What a beautiful thought. Wouldn't it be amazing if that's the way the world was?

Leaving Cambodia and saying good-bye is not going to be easy for me. These are such good, warm, hardworking people. I will miss everyone I have met here.

I am now on my way to Bangkok, where I will spend the

night at an airport hotel. Then early the following morning I return to Los Angeles.

Friday, July 27

I woke up shaking and sweating after having a recurring nightmare—the same one I had in Phnom Penh. I know what it is now: I am remembering what I saw at the Genocide Museum. I woke up so scared and uncomfortable I couldn't breathe, just like I couldn't breathe in those cells. Marie-Noëlle told me she had the same feeling when we were there. We continue to be haunted by one afternoon in that prison.

There are so many Cambodians over a certain age who will remember everything. I don't know how they live on. But they do, with so much strength of will and power and spirit. They are an example to us all.

The last picture in the photo insert was taken two years after my Cambodian journal was written. My life changed; this country, Cambodia, has had a profound effect on me. In this picture, my son Maddox and I are returning home again to Cambodia. We now live in Samlot. Sarath, from the CVD, and I have started an animal sanctuary. The land mine victims he introduced me to have become close friends and we are now neighbors. Our children play together. We also work together on housing and farming projects.

I was most honored when a year ago Moon and his wife, who had married in a Thai refugee camp, wanted to remarry.

They lost their parents in the war and so Moon asked me to represent his mother in the ceremony. I was extremely honored and proud to be there. It was a beautiful day. Cambodian weddings are traditionally loud and long. Even in the poorest of villages they still are very elaborate.

One part of the ceremony was to put string rope around the arms of the bride and groom. Moon, who lost his arms at his elbows and his vision from a land mine, had black plastic sunglasses on during the wedding. When they tried to wrap rope around her wrists and his upper arm there were smiles and laughter from the children.

Past the sadness and self-pity these people accept the reality of their lives and are grateful for all they have. I am proud to call these people friends and excited to raise my son—proud of his people—proud to be a Cambodian.

Mission to Pakistan

During August 17 through August 26, 2001, I undertook a mission on behalf of UNHCR to visit Afghan refugees in Pakistan.

Friday, August 17

I leave tomorrow for Pakistan. On purpose, I have waited until now to begin to read in depth about what is happening there and in neighboring Afghanistan, where people are fleeing for their lives.

It is a shame how, for a time, I can so easily shut out the world's problems when I am safe at home.

I notice some articles in the newspapers I read, but they are usually focused on current emergency situations. They don't present a story so many years old. Perhaps to them it seems hopeless, and even worse, not urgent. It is not newsworthy. Old stories become facts of life. They become accepted situations. The people in these countries will simply live with and die from some horrible situation. I read how almost two million people are in Pakistan living as refugees. They live along the borders. They live with nothing.

I read about a German-based relief organization that had twenty-four of its workers arrested by the Taliban. Their office was closed. They were there to help the refugees, but they were accused of propagating Christianity.

The fate of the twenty-four people, eight of whom are foreigners, is still unknown. I hope by the time someone reads this the outcome has not been their death.

This will be the first trip I am allowing a video camera with me. As uncomfortable about that as I am, I know what I have seen before on these missions, and my pen falls short. I can't tell people what it is like to sit with wounded men and abandoned women and children all hungry and desperately trying to survive, holding on to what is left of their dignity, their self-worth, their hope. They are the people you cry for and the people who give you strength.

They understand something about life that many of us (thank God) never will, and they focus on many things we have forgotten. They know what to be grateful for. They appreciate the importance of family and community. They understand the power of faith and love.

I just started to read more facts. I don't know what to write or what I feel. I know I can't believe what I am reading. I don't understand how these things are possible today.

Saturday, August 18

At 8:40 P.M. I leave for London (ten hours).

Then I have a two-hour layover.

Then it's another eight and a half hours to Islamabad.

Monday, August 20

As we began our descent into Islamabad, we heard over the speaker:

"Take your antimalaria pills. Aerial photography of Pakistan is not allowed. Bringing in alcohol is prohibited."

At 4:32 A.M. I arrived in Islamabad, Pakistan.

I met Yusuf Hassan at the gate, a UNHCR (United Nations Commissioner for Refugees) officer. He is from Kenya.

I am told, "Men will not shake a woman's hand. It is best not to make eye contact with men. Cover your head with a shawl. We will be shopping for appropriate clothing for you. A plain-dressed armed official will always be with us."

Hearing all this, I can't help but ask myself, why am I here?

But I

I am told in Afghanistan is not allowed to employ women. are allowed only very little contact with women—so to help is very difficult. I am now guarded and veiled, surrounded and attended to politely. I already feel a little uncomfortable, like a princess under guard. I am used to such independence and freedom.

UNHCR Office—Islamabad

Everyone at the UNHCR office is kind and welcoming.

This office was once a warehouse. There are so many filing cabinets filled with records of the refugees.

At this time, Pakistan hosts over two million Afghan refugees. I am told that what must be remembered is "there is no peace in sight."

Many of these refugees have been here for twenty-two years, since Russia invaded Afghanistan in 1979. Toward the back of the office-warehouse are barbed wire fences. Very few people are allowed in. I see rows of quiet women waiting. The men are yelling. I caught the eyes of a man. He looked angry. I am told there have been times the angry, frustrated refugees have broken in.

The UNHCR officers can only complete about twenty interviews a day. It seems so little when you think about the 2.3 million refugees here in this country, but helping to save twenty families each day is a great accomplishment.

Being registered is the first step toward someone hearing their story and a chance for a better life.

10 A.M.

I am being driven to the market to buy the rest of the appropriate clothing I must wear while I am here. One of the jobs refugee children have here, and all around the world, is to collect trash to try to find usable things.

We stopped at a red light. A boy of about six years old knocks on my window. He shows me his amputated arm. I have been told not to give money to those who beg. If possible, give food instead. Many children are being sent out by their parents to beg.

About half the people in Pakistan go to bed hungry every night.

This child looks into my eyes. He is just a little boy. I pass him something through the window. At the next light, an older man on crutches approaches our car.

It is so hot and crowded. I don't know how people work outside all day, and they all seem to work very hard.

In this intense heat, it is hard for me to imagine being without water, but with the drought that has been going on here and in neighboring areas for the last four years, many people have had little or no access to water.

Pakistan has a very decorative culture. The buses are amazing with elaborate, colorful details. Paintings and metal sculptures are attached to them. The clothes are more colorful than I had imagined they would be, though they are still modest in how much they cover.

The first place we stopped was the shoe shop.

The shoes are handcrafted, and I am still not sure if there is a left and a right. Some shoes look like they are right out of *Aladdin*, with gold and silver toes that point up.

Once we are back, I shower and try to nap—but I can't sleep. I try to call home. No one is there.

I have learned that no country in the world wants to give Afghanistan help because of the Taliban, and it is hard to get goods past the Taliban to the innocent who are in such desperate need. Aside from the need for food and water, there are also land mines that need to be destroyed. So many innocent people are suffering.

I met with Abbas Sarfraz Khan, the minister responsible for refugee affairs.

I didn't know where to sit; do I cover my head or not? I

have heard he is Westernized. He attended college in Boston. He has also lived in London. He offered me a drink. I said, "No, thank you." Monserrat (a UNHCR staff member) whispered to me, "Order something—green tea."

The minister spoke of:

- the generations with no education
- the lack of awareness in the West
- donor fatigue

Upon leaving I was relieved when he reached his hand out to shake mine. I wasn't sure if that was okay.

As an American, I feel I was not raised to seriously think outside my own country—to appreciate and to learn about other cultures. America is not alone in this—many countries do not focus their students or people on other cultures.

12:30 P.M.

We are on our way to visit a shelter for Pakistani and Afghan women. It is also a place where they can go to get counseling about domestic violence.

The tents are just sticks with sheets over them. (Occasional areas are used for all the poor—not just the refugees.) At the shelter I was brought into a room full of women who all had their heads covered and their shoes off.

We visit Sach, a women's group whose purpose is to struggle for change. Sach means truth in Urdu. So far 100 women have been training with Sach. All of them have started small businesses in the Sunday markets.

I asked the Afghan women, "Would you want to be resettled back in Afghanistan?"

One woman's response was, "We want to be where we can be safe and free. You tell us."

Another woman hands me a photo. "This is my son, who the Taliban killed."

A woman with a shaky voice and tearful eyes moves forward. Her name is kept private as promised. She fears for her safety. Her brother is disabled and can no longer work for his family because of the severe beating he received from the Taliban.

Another woman showed me a paper, and it was explained to me that it was a bill for four guns. This was a tax she had to pay to support the war effort. She had sold all she had to give to the Taliban, but it was still not enough to buy the four guns.

A woman who was a doctor said one night the Taliban came to her house. She escaped to the neighbors, but her father was arrested and jailed. She is alone. She does not know if her father is still alive. She has also converted to Christianity, which gives her more reason to be scared of the Taliban. If they found out she would be condemned to death. She is still being hunted. She has to move often so they cannot find her. Even though she is in Pakistan she is still in danger of being killed. A UNHCR staff member wants to know why she has not come to the UNHCR office. They desperately want her to get in touch.

A man is welcomed into the room. He wants to share. He

brought his wife and children to this center because they are malnourished. The man also seemed very shaky as he spoke. He had sweet eyes. Sadly, they were bright yellow. He was badly beaten by the Taliban. His legs are partially numb and his kidneys are severely damaged.

Urban Refugees

We take a drive to a slum area near a bus terminal and a fruit market. The poor people live here so they can live off the thrown-away—mostly rotten—food.

This is a very sad area that includes much commercial sexual exploitation of children. I have been told the children sell their bodies for the equivalent of five cents.

Sach is working here to help the children. Many of them are as young as six years old. They are taken into the sex trade and other abusive situations.

There are more programs here trying to teach children's rights.

A woman tells me many mothers have six to twelve children who work in the sex trade. These parents are desperate. These children have no schooling, no childhood, no protection.

I went for a walk. There are dirt paths between the little mud houses.

I saw a little girl around four years old carrying a large pile of wood on her head. So many other little girls are carrying their baby brothers and sisters on their hips. I notice a few of these girls have obvious skin diseases. I pass a schoolroom with no lights. There is no electricity anywhere in this mud village.

No one is allowed to even talk about AIDS here. AIDS is a taboo subject. Different organizations are trying to introduce AIDS awareness and sex education.

Sach Rehabilitation and Training Center

This is where women come who will be resettled. Someone says they are the lucky ones. They have been chosen because of their serious sexual abuse and because they have no husbands.

They receive twenty-four-hour medical coverage. The center is secured by Brinks Security.

The women running this program are very strong. Stones were thrown at them when they proposed to build a school. The rooms are very small. In one little bed there can be two or three small children with their mother. One woman I met is receiving psychiatric help. She was raped and beaten bloody by the Taliban. She can't remember too much. She has three children.

I notice a poster on the wall referring to the sex trafficking of missing women and children.

74 MILLION WOMEN MISSING
IN SOUTH ASIA
INDIA — PAKISTAN — THE PHILIPPINES

Another poster from a Cambodian sister organization reads:

WOMEN DON'T BELONG
IN CAGES

Eighty percent of imprisoned women are inside for poverty-related offenses.

Ninety percent of aboriginal and 82 percent of all women in prison are survivors of incest, rape, or physical assault.

This message is written on the board:

"IF WE ALL DO A LITTLE,
WE CAN DO A LOT."

A few of these families will be resettled in the United States, but we have to bring their expectations down before they attempt to start their new life. I look at the little kids' faces. Will they be welcomed? Called names? If you or I saw them next month on a U.S. street would we even try to imagine or understand what they might have been through?

7 P.M.

We had dinner at Monserrat's home. There were about fifteen people from UNHCR, the American Embassy, the ministry of Pakistan, and a woman from the BBC. It continues to amaze me when I sit in on a dinner like this. It is always inspiring. All everyone speaks of all night long are global issues, humanitarian needs, etc. They share their information, discuss solutions, and plan on ways to work together. These people are from all different parts of the world—brought together by a shared desire to help people in need, to help end suffering. There were heavy moments and moments of laughter. Sometimes I get scared when everyone talks politics, but I didn't this time. What I learned tonight was that the observations and feelings of an individual who is trying to understand are just as important. I also realized while I was talking that I have learned more than I thought. But to make sense of it all—no one can.

- that some people are not treated as equal
- that people go to bed hungry
- that millions of people are experiencing persecution, human-rights violations, and conflict

No one can make sense of it because it makes no sense.

Tuesday, August 21—6 A.M. On the Road to Jalozai Camp

I am told I may run into an American delegation. I asked why they would be there. I was told it is to see for themselves in order to make decisions about what needs to be done or what can continue.

I am also told it is most likely about whether or not to allow more people to be resettled in the United States. Today they allow 1,000 per year to resettle. They could double that number—at least that is the hope. I know probably many people in my country feel 1,000 is too high—even if it is nothing when you consider the millions of people at risk.

What is the answer?

Where do these people belong?

The answer is always to have peace at home—in their country of origin. Sometimes it seems impossible. Pakistan and Iran are very poor countries where millions of refugees have been living for twenty years.

It is explained to me that two things are necessary to help more people.

1. The numbers allowed in host countries must increase.
2. The staff needs funding, assistance, and manpower to process and handle twice the caseload.

Outside the window I see mosques (Muslim temples). They stand out amidst the rubble, makeshift tents, and mud buildings.

The buffalo and cows on the side of the road are fat in comparison to those I have seen in other countries.

Painted buses move through the streets. The dress uniform on men and women is different than I had imagined. There is something elegant about them. Some have very vibrant colors with small mirrors and embroidery sewn on them. Some, however, seem like uniforms.

The roads are smooth. I am told the infrastructure is good. We drive beside horse-drawn carts. The horses seem little and skinny. It makes me wonder if animal-rights activists would be upset—probably just sad. It's strange how sometimes it seems some people care more for their animals than the poor family next door.

As I write this I am sitting alone in the car. Others are behind in the second UNHCR truck. The police pulled us over and said we were speeding, but there are no speed limit signs, and all the cars that continue to pass us are going so much faster.

Here, the police don't pull up behind you. They stand at the side of the road and stick out a stop sign. I didn't want to write while they were talking to the drivers outside the car. The other policemen were watching us. I'm not sure what they wanted. To scare us? Or try to get money? There was a lot of heavy talk and it seems nothing was accomplished. Twenty minutes later we were on the road again. As we get closer to the Shamshatoo refugee camp, many Afghan women are completely covered with only little holes around their eyes to look out.

We stop at a little market in "little Kabul" (a slice of Afghanistan). Enterprising people have been trading here for twenty years.

There is something magical about these people. It also seems like I have gone back in time. It feels like Biblical times only with dusty piles of glass bottles and trucks with modern wheels and horns.

Jalozai Camp Site—Briefing

UNHCR set up and funded this camp.

Médecins Sans Frontières—Doctors Without Borders (MSF) is here to provide health care.

Catholic Relief Services (CRS), a nongovernmental organization (NGO), is also here helping to provide health services and sanitation facilities (over 1,000 dry pit latrines). They also distribute blankets, quilts, and mattresses to the refugees.

There are two main reasons for Afghans fleeing:

1. In Northern Afghanistan, there is fighting between the Taliban and the Northern Alliance.
2. The three-year drought.

We drive through the camp to a point inside where we will get out and hopefully talk with people.

We pass by a few little boys. They smile and wave at our trucks. They all recognize the U.N. by now (they have been present here over twenty years).

Many women are completely covered. They can see you, but you can't see them. Even little girls are covered up. All except for their eyes. It makes me immediately focus my attention on their gaze. Most of them seem curious, but others just stare. I feel intimidated by these people—even the children. They are strong-minded survivors with a strong faith.

We pass the little mud houses, which appear to be ten to fifteen years old.

Suddenly there is a sea of tents (ranging from fabric to canvas to plastic).

I think of gypsies.

This whole area is extremely hot and very dusty. There is very little shelter from the sun. Water trucks have had to be brought in. World Health Organization (WHO) is here to help. On July 18 there were many deaths because of heat (125 degrees Fahrenheit) and dehydration.

A little boy in line had purple spots and scabs on his face. It is polio-immunization day. Many children are waiting in tents. Along the sidewall of a big tent, old army cots are covered with flies. In this area the local clinics do not have very much. They do not have the ability to take on any serious medical needs. But the health center is open twenty-four hours a day.

"Water supplies have gotten better. There has been less diarrhea and dysentery. There is also TB control. But even when something seems to be under control—there are constant new arrivals."

There was a deforming condition called leishmaniasis. They got medicine from Geneva.

The health clinic has been at the camp for nine months, but only in the last month did they receive a generator.

Forms of birth control (family planning) have been introduced. Birth control is almost impossible in urban areas. So it is amazing that they are breaking through to the people in the camp.

I met a child whose mother told me he was four years old, but he looked to be the size of an infant. Looking at his face I can see he is a boy. His facial features are not those of a baby. He became this way because of years of malnutrition. The clinic here has him on a program. I look around and see so many children who need to be monitored.

An hour later, I am back in the car. The same people who gathered around us as we walked the camps are now watching us leave. There are so many sick children. As we are leaving, I see a little boy about five years old who has abscesses on his face—four of them the size of golf balls. A doctor who was going to travel with us to the next area is now staying here to operate immediately on him.

No permanent structures are allowed here by the Pakistani government. They say they are fed up with all the burden sharing. I visit a school. Kids are shouting the alphabet. They are all boys. Girls are on different mats than the boys. The girls are shouting numbers.

Many young children are coughing. I notice many have heat rashes. I met one little girl in an old pink faded torn dress. Her words were interpreted for me. She talked with the wisdom of a forty-year-old woman.

"They bombarded my house. They attacked my house with guns and bombs. They cut off my uncle's legs and killed two of my cousins."

I am guessing the Taliban, but I don't ask. Instead, I ask what she wants. What are her needs?

"I want peace. I want to go back to Afghanistan. I want to go home."

I ask how long has she been here.

"Nine months living under plastic."

I was taken to the screening center for registration. I saw many children lying on the ground trying to find shade. Men in berets with large rifles guarded the area. We are in a frontier province just on the Afghan-Pakistani border. I met a very nice Irish lady, a lawyer for the refugees working with UNHCR.

A woman was brought in during our briefing. She lost her identification slip. Her only ID was a food card. She had no family. I was told UNHCR will try to get other information to help her replace the identification card. Registration is now into the third week. It is a very organized program. They have managed to screen over 7,000 families, a total of about 42,000 people. All refugees are asked if they would like the option to repatriate. If they do, they will get assistance back to Afghanistan as well as a package of 150 kilos of wheat and also money equivalent to about $90 American dollars.

Still, I don't understand the option of repatriation, when there is fear of the Taliban, fighting in the north, and the ground is covered with land mines. Afghanistan is one of the top two most mine-covered countries in the world.

I am now in a room where a woman is being interviewed. She desperately wants to go back to Afghanistan, where her relatives have chosen to return. She knows it is a war zone, and still she says, "What will I do here by myself?"

She has her veil lifted. I guess it is okay because she is in the company of women.

Of the 7,000 families screened over the past three weeks, only six families have chosen to return to Afghanistan.

New arrivals are screened daily. If they are recognized as refugees they will be sent to the next camp. This camp, the Shamshatoo refugee camp, was established in 1998. This particular camp started with 300 families—now there are 3,000 families living there.

On our way out, officers were approached by an unaccompanied child. He was about ten years old and said he has a younger sister and brother. In New Jalozai the number of widows and orphans is extremely high.

It is very hot here. I want to take off this outfit. I am offered a small paper cup of water. I don't ask for more. We drive out through a small mass of about eighty people who have gathered to watch us leave. Their faces are red from the heat.

Shelter Now International (SNI)

This is the same NGO that had twenty-four people taken, accused of preaching Christianity: sixteen local Afghans and eight international aid workers.

SNI runs the kitchen here.

I saw the medical center, the vocation center, and the food-distribution center. They also have a child-to-child group here where children teach children.

I met Peter, an official in this refugee camp. He is Australian. He introduces me to the boys and girls.

I also met Shaifullah, a ten-year-old boy with a beautiful face. It was clear and kind. I asked him a few questions.

"Do you teach your brothers and sisters?"

"Yes—family first."

"Do you have a message for the world?"

Before he answers he giggles and hides his smile under a cloth, too shy to answer. Then he looked up and said, "Peace in Afghanistan."

World Food Program (WFP) is in this camp today distributing flour, lentils, and edible oil. The refugees receive this once a month. I am in the medical office—the basic health unit for the camp.

Polio days are from the 21st to the 23rd for all children under five years old. There are three teams in the field today. There are five basic health units here all funded by UNHCR. Vaccination materials are from UNICEF.

Vocational Training Center

Occupational training is offered, mainly for the disabled. Over each tented booth are signs: masonry, carpentry, shoemaking, and tinsmith.

Two children are learning shoemaking. Their father lost his arm in a land mine accident, so the children have to learn to support their family.

I try to buy a pair of shoes, but they insist on giving them to me. Then I ask, "How much for a pair for my husband?" I want to buy something from them. They respond with, "No money will be exchanged between us here. We promote goodwill and humanitarian deeds. That is the payment."

These programs are funded by UNHCR through Jamalludin Afghan (a famous Afghan nongovernmental organization). The length of the training courses is six months per person.

We then go to meet women and children at the community center. The men traveling with us are not allowed in the room.

Youth Club and Female Welfare Committee

Inside.

"*Asalaamu alaykum.*" Happiest I've seen them. Smiles.

The women were calling me "Angelina *Bibi*." (*Bibi* is a word of respect for a woman.)

They discuss family violence and talk about how to deal with it. They are learning their human rights as women and children.

One year ago they were living in plastic tents and having many more problems than they have today. They are doing much better. They have built small mud homes. They make jokes. They worry because food distribution is sometimes late. "We become desperate because we are big families."

I met two young mothers with their babies. One child was mentally challenged. The other one was sick. Like most mothers around the world, they were very loving and sweet to their babies. Here with all that is happening they are very concerned for their families. They are scared.

The sick baby has an itchy rash. She has big, brown eyes. She keeps staring at me. Her mother stands her up and shows me boils on her back from the heat.

They told me about a six-year-old girl who was raped, suffocated, and then put in a latrine. Her mother did not want to tell the police for fear of having difficulties in the future. I asked this woman if she had a message for me to bring back to America.

"We want peace in Afghanistan."

Another woman I met told me her husband died of heatstroke. She also spoke very strongly to me—looking at me. Her words were translated for me. "What would you do if this happened to you? What would you do? Our life is finished. It is gone. But our children have no future—our children must have a future."

Hearing this I couldn't help but start to cry. She then asked me to "please remember us and our families."

I move on to a young girls' group. Four different girls give me a beaded pin, a hair band, and embroidery. It is a customary way to treat a guest. It is the Afghan culture.

Like the others, this camp is also very hot. There is no electricity. The camp security is not very good.

The girls are not learning vocational training—only basic skills women teach each other.

They want to learn more. They are eager to learn more, but mostly they just sit and embroider, and sew, and make jewelry (for no pay). They want jobs so they can buy more food for their families. They want to feel they are working to make things better.

But before food distribution, housing programs, vocational training, and child care, there must be protection. UNHCR gives them the protection they need. Funding must be increased, and awareness must be higher.

3 P.M.

We check into a local hotel. Mr. Ahmad, my security officer (gunman), insisted on going in first to inspect my room. He looked around thoroughly and he also looked out the window. "It's okay."

Mr. Ahmad has been with me since my arrival. He keeps a polite distance most of the time, unless there is a need for protection. I don't see or understand what he sees when he looks around an area we are in. Yesterday in the middle of the market he suddenly rushed me back to the car. I never asked why. I don't question him. I know there is much I don't understand here. And as an outsider, I am blind too.

"If anyone knocks on your door do not answer it. Call me. I am in the room right across from you."

We had dinner with the local UNHCR staff. A man in uniform with a gun opened the door. Everyone took their shoes off before entering the room. We all sat on pillows.

Even with a small air conditioner and an extra fan, it was still very hot. They also tell me this is not one of their hotter days. Every so often I felt like I was going to pass out. It is easy to understand the deaths caused by heat.

In the wintertime—in the plastic tents—many people (especially children) freeze to death overnight. And during the hot days the tents can become like ovens. Too horrible to think about.

Wednesday, August 22

Up at 6:30 A.M. this morning.

First stop—UNHCR Peshawar office for a briefing in which I learned that two-thirds of the refugee population goes back twenty years.

In one of the large camps in this area, the day of June 30 has been given as the eviction date for many refugees.

Now after negotiations with the UNHCR, the Pakistani government has given them until the 30 of September. After twenty years and millions of refugees inside their borders they are starting to want them out, even if—as we know—out is to the Taliban land mines.

To give time for screening. To try to save as many refugees from being deported as they can and to find a place for them.

I notice stacks of papers each with a black-and-white passport-size photo.

Roy Herrmann shows me around. I am brought into different rooms. It is very early, but everyone seems very busy, and I don't want to waste a moment of their time. We are supposed to fly to Quetta at 4 P.M., but we are told to watch the weather. If it rains, there is a good chance we won't take off.

The office is modest. The rooms are filled with files and books. There are fans but it is still very warm inside. There are one hundred applications per day, but only four or five a day can be processed. More help is needed here. There have been cutbacks and a lack of funds for UNHCR.

Center for Street Children and Beggar Women

At this center, there are more refugees in urban areas.

UNHCR can only cover refugees in camps. So in urban areas there is no government support. Through NGOs and local help is how urban areas are assisted. UNHCR does support a few of the NGOs.

I see twenty kids on the floor, girls and boys mixed in different rows. This is not a formal school.

There is another room of children in a language class learning *Dari*. I am told by my interpreter, "They want to sing a song of welcoming for you."

These children are so poor, and yet they smile and sing. Their faces are so serious, so focused on their songs.

Some of the children have very serious visible scars. They all miss Afghanistan and want to go back.

When the children came here they were malnourished—a lot of vitamin deficiencies. They were fourteen-year-old boys who looked so much younger. They are learning carpentry and welding. They also want to be engravers and doctors.

A teacher says, "They have high hopes."

Nasir Bagh Camp

These people will be forced to leave soon. UNHCR negotiated time for screening to pull out the most vulnerable before they are evicted.

This community will be completely destabilized.

The refugees at the screening center—over a hundred—are waiting outside. They are aware of their situation and they are getting restless.

I keep my eyes down as I walk in, not because I feel threatened or uncomfortable as a woman, but because I feel helpless and ashamed. Many women want only women in the interview room. They seem desperate to be registered with their group and want to be in the same convoy. They want to be together if they have to start over in a new area.

No one wants to be left on their own.

School in Camp

The kids are not here today. I met with four teachers, one man and three women. One of the women was holding a baby. She has been teaching here for eight years. So much work has been put into this camp over the years to become a community—however modest.

There are maps on the walls for the children. In total there are twenty teachers at this school. There are 3,000 students (1,000 boys and 2,000 girls). This is one of the largest schools for Afghan refugee girls.

I ask their feelings about September (the month a large part of their camp is set to be demolished). Up to the last day, they say it is best to keep going to school. They will stay as long as they can. They are hoping to eventually set up "shift schools" where the bulk of these refugees will be sent when they are evacuated. The room we are sitting in now is in the area that is set to be demolished.

Then I visited a small day house at the camp.

These women do not want to repatriate back to Afghanistan. They would not be allowed to be educated. Employment for women is also banned. Most of all, they are afraid of the Taliban—afraid for their families.

I stand to the side and watch. How can I speak for these people? I know nothing of hunger and war. In the corner I see two small children making a carpet. A mother explains that back home they would be in nursery school. Can you imagine, being a parent, having to force your small children to work? They watch their children get sick in these camps from so much dust. They have allergies and serious coughs.

They do want us to know that they are very thankful to the Pakistani government for their hospitality. I met another woman with four small children. She works in the medical center for $40 a month. She does not want to go back to Afghanistan. She will no longer be allowed to work.

The women invited us to stay for lunch. If we did, we would be taking part of their already limited rations. We said, "Thank you but we are on a schedule and unfortunately have no time for lunch." As we were slowly driving away, several little children gathered around the car.

They wave and say, "Bye-bye!"

One little one wipes the dust off the window to look through. She smiles at me. I put my hands up against the glass. She matches my hands finger for finger.

I feel I should give them something, but I don't have enough of anything to give to all of them. I do have three bracelets and a scarf, but as I am thinking that, I realize they are not looking or wanting me to give them anything. They just seem happy to have a new visitor—someone who smiles at them and who is willing to play a little.

As we left, the children ran alongside the car—running barefoot in the dirt and rocks. One girl falls. I look back. She is fine. A little boy is helping her. She is smiling.

We drive to an area that is already in the process of being demolished. All windows, doors, and wood boards have been removed. So far, 1,042 families from this camp have been repatriated.

There was intense pressure. Some were forced to go back. In this area, the poor Pakistani people will benefit when this land that they have shared is returned to them. For over twenty years they have been sharing this area—their home—with refugees. The international community should not expect them to carry so much of the burden. It is a very complicated situation, but put simply, both refugees and host countries are affected by war. Refugees are very grateful to the host countries. I feel we should help host countries not just to make refugee programs run well, but also to thank them, to acknowledge all the people living in the host country, and to show deep gratitude to them and their government.

But in regard to Pakistan, it is complicated. Many Pakistanis feel they are responsible because the Taliban originated here. A man says to me, "It's like raising an alligator that grows up to eat you."

We stop at a refugee camp cemetery. It seems to go on for miles. There are newly dug graves. I am told they are mostly children.

Many families fled to Pakistan carrying dead bodies to give them a burial here. Talking with the families I would ask them how difficult it is to be given the news of forced repatriation. These people built a new life, and now, they will have to tear down, move, and start over. They have no words. One woman starts to cry.

I am told it is also very hard for UNHCR staff. They are often forced to rotate and not stay in one place too long. It is often emotionally hard to stay professional (objective).

Sayyed Jamalludin

This is an Afghan Welfare Organization Center funded by UNHCR for vocational training. They help train and look after about 400 refugees a year. As soon as we entered the area a man passed by using all four limbs to walk. He had shoes on his hands. He has extreme polio. The most vulnerable are the disabled.

I don't know how they are working in this extreme heat. Most of these people are either amputees or paralyzed (men and women).

People here work very hard, and what they make is amazing. Aside from the movable library, they make shoes, windowpanes, and even stoves.

After visiting for a while we are offered shade and a soda—Pepsi in glass bottles from a dusty crate. It was very generous of them to give us these Pepsis. We drink—not wanting to waste a drop. We visit a class of twelve-year-old boys who were illiterate but are now learning to read. Next, we see a roomful of girls practicing their beginning reading skills. It is so exciting to see these children being given access to an education.

One woman said to us, "God bless you for all your help. Without it we would have tied hands." These woman are so strong. Their eyes smile through their veils.

Haji, the man who has been showing us around, said, "Thank you and God bless you for leaving your comfortable life to visit us and spend time with us."

As we drive away, I notice more groups of women fully covered. The full-body and head-covered clothing, with several tiny holes over the eyes, is called a burquah.

In Iran it is black. In Pakistan it is usually white. In Afghanistan it is usually blue. No one can make eye contact with each other. Children cannot see their mother's expressions.

No individuality—no self—and it is very hot. I bought one and tried it on. I felt like I was in a cage. They are horrible.

Thursday, August 23

Up at 6:30 A.M. this morning.

I had a talk with Yusuf over coffee about the frustrations, the lack of funding, and the program cutbacks.

We also discuss how sad the misconception people have of refugees is and how little they want to have them in their community.

We need to change the perception of refugees. They deserve respect.

We must open up our eyes to the wonderful diversity in this world.

Quetta Briefing

There are fifteen staff here—four international. Veronique is from Nigeria.

We went around the room introducing ourselves and explaining what we do.

Six months ago I started to travel with UNHCR and began learning about refugees, people living in "man-made misery."

I tell them the countries I have visited: Afghanistan, Sierra Leone, Cambodia.

I look around this roomful of tired faces. A woman says, "We are all doing the best we can." She is from Africa and has been here helping for almost a year.

One of the women with us, Serena, has been working in this office since 1983. I am honored to know and work with the people of UNHCR. They are good people. They so desperately want to help all of the refugees but they are so underfunded. With every cutback, so many people suffer. The reality is that lives depend on every dollar given to UNHCR.

We drive one hour to a refugee camp called New Saranan.

During the drive I see camels, elaborately decorated buses, barbed wire fences, and dusty people curled up in the only spots of shade they can find. I learn that as a people, Afghans are agriculturalists. They are enterprising, hardworking people. They live in the middle of nowhere with practically nothing, and yet they find ways to be creative and artistic. In their little art market, donkey carts carry their work and sometimes also fruit.

Inside the car, they reach over me to make sure my door is locked.

I realize I hardly see any women anywhere.

We pass the market. I can see new areas containing refugees with no shelter in sight. There is also no shade and no water. I notice a little boy with a stick and two small goats.

How are these people surviving? I see how little they live

with, but they make use of all that they do have. Everything is precious. I keep thinking of how much I waste at home and of how much more I have than I need (water, food, clothes, and so on).

New Saranan Refugee Camp

All of the camps in Pakistan appear as if they are all one and the same. They all contain:

- a world built of dust
- dirt roads
- mud homes and tents

The camp is seven to eight kilometers long. The only water source is seventeen kilometers away. When I stepped out of the car there was dust everywhere. I could feel it in my eyes and throat.

We stop at the medical center. It consists of very small rooms with old tables and dusty carpets. They practice physiotherapy here. The main illnesses are polio, bone TB, burns, land mine injuries, bullet wounds, and trauma. Over 50 percent of the patients here are children under five years old.

There is a room for women. Three women lie face to floor on old mats. They have no use of their legs. They try to lift up and stretch their backs for exercise.

Outside I meet an Afghan man with a white beard. His wife was blinded and his two sons were killed. Here at Saranan camp there is no funding for training skills for the handicapped.

Another man tells me his story. He lost one arm and an eye.

Some people complain and say UNHCR should do more to help the refugees. This is hard for the staff to hear. These people simply don't understand the limited funds and cutbacks.

As one staff member said, "People can complain about us around the world, and governments can criticize our programs, but every day we continue to come face-to-face with hungry, sick people who feel it is up to us to help them."

How can I explain this? Maybe it's like there are a group of people in a car and a group of starving war-wounded people standing outside alongside the car. A few people (UNHCR, humanitarian aid workers, etc.) get out of the car and give all they have, but it is not enough to help everyone. And then the remaining starving people become difficult to deal with. Some people never even leave the car. They don't attempt to solve problems, can't solve the problems, and don't want to be attacked. When things seem overwhelming, many people simply do nothing.

We walk on through the camp—

Two women are giving polio vaccinations. One baby is crying. Most of the little kids understand, and they are willingly stepping forward. It is such a simple vaccination—a few drops in the mouth. It means the difference of whether or not these children will have use of their limbs in the future. Without these agencies, these people would suffer even more in their lives from preventable diseases.

Ten million refugee children under the age of five die each year, the majority from preventable diseases and malnutrition.

We visit a room where young women are studying. The men we are traveling with remain outside as we go in.

The girls stand. They want to recite "A Poem for Education" for us. You want to cry. To see these young women wanting so much to have a better life and a chance to learn.

There are some math problems on the board that I can't solve.

They bring us a soda—each a different kind—all that is available. I notice one of the small tin libraries on wheels in the corner.

I ask them what they want to be when they grow up. Many of the girls have the same answer—a doctor. One girl says, "If we work very hard we can."

I ask what the most difficult thing about living in this camp is.

"There are not enough jobs." (Which is so strange to hear from girls so young.)

"We need water. Even with trucks. Still not enough water."

I ask through the translator, "Do you want to go back to Afghanistan?" They all answer at the same time—"Yes."

I ask, "Why can't you go back now?"

"They are fighting in our country." "We are not allowed to have an education there."

An older woman comes in. She said, "Before the Taliban, women in big cities were able to get an education." She is so happy to see schoolrooms like this—even though they are in refugee camps.

Some of these girls also teach the younger small children. The girls stand and smile sweetly as we say good-bye. We step out again into the dust. The heat is overwhelming. We move on to a crowded little room where several older women are learning.

The room is about fifteen feet by eight feet. The walls are made of mud, the ceiling is made of twigs. There are little square holes for windows. These women are learning to write. A woman shows me she can write her name. She is so happy. "Now I can write a letter to my family."

A small boy peeks in the windows. He has a haunting face. He watches us. I think, Maybe his mother is here in the room. The women say that the best benefit of education is that they can share their knowledge with others. When family planning and safe sex is mentioned they become shy and smile and laugh. It is awkward for them. One of the women, who is recently married, covers her face playfully when asked if she knows about these issues.

They want us to take a picture of them. "Can you send us a copy? We want our families to see us in school." It was wonderful talking with them.

Once outside we stood for a few minutes against the shady side of the wall. Young boys and a few officers with rifles stood nearby.

I haven't been able to write in about an hour. I am feeling nauseous. I need water. Maybe that will make me feel better.

We drive to the next area. We are passing little old canvas tents, but it is so dusty, it is hard to see them. It looks like the end of the world—a forgotten place. How do people live there?

Another hour passes. We are in the mountains on curvy roads—nothing but dust and rocks surround us. We pass a bus overcrowded with people.

The air conditioner in our truck seems to be blowing hot air. I find myself daydreaming about my refrigerator and the cool breeze I feel when the sliding doors are open in my kitchen. I know that must sound stupid, but it's the truth. Your mind wanders in the heat. I have to focus on something else. It helps me from feeling sick.

I think about what is happening to all these people here— so much overwhelming sadness. I feel helpless. This situation is hell on earth, but the people—the people are magic and inspiring. They work so hard to survive.

We pass an area with a few mud houses and fruit trees— which is probably their only source of income. There are clear signs that every part of this land has been affected by the drought.

We pass a truck full of cut-down trees. They must sell the wood. One of the workers tells me, "It will take seven years for those trees to grow again, and they will only grow when the drought ends." Unless these people receive financial aid, this will be another area of people with no future. We drive by a refugee camp that was closed due to a lack of resources. They were moved to another camp. We stop where the camp was torn down. I see a few families who have stayed and are living in the rubble. I see only women and children.

Little barefooted boys run out to see us. They are so young and yet they have a heavy sadness in their faces. They are all terribly thin and their tummies are slightly swollen. They play on a ground of nothing but sharp rocks and patches of cracked dry earth.

We give them bottles of water from the ice box we carry with us on this journey. I thought it was silly when they boarded it on our small plane. Now I understand. So much needs to be considered in places like this.

We see a family of women walk over. This empty camp looks like the ruins of an old civilization.

I ask one of the women, "Is it okay if we are here?"

She answers, "Why not? God should bring more guests."

One of the women is pregnant. She has blue tribal tattoos on her face and is wearing colorful jewelry.

These women tell us they came from Afghanistan in 1979. I ask why.

"Because of the war with Russia. We left our houses and irrigated land. Now—there is Taliban—we can't go back." They invite us into a little room where they lay out an old, dusty quilt.

I ask if there is a hospital nearby. They look at me like "How could that be?"

I notice a little boy who looks very sad. He has torn clothes and big watery eyes. He is making such an effort to smile.

I ask if they know about America.

"Yes—our men tell us America helps us."

I ask them if they have a message for America.

"Why must we suffer?" "Why are we so desperate?" "We are grateful for America's help, but please—we need more food and water and we wish no more deaths."

We ask if it is all right to take their picture.

"No, our men will be upset." We understand. But they do ask us to please take a picture of the children.

The little boy seems scared. "He has never seen a camera."

We talk about the food shortage. "My family can only afford one bag a month. We are trying to teach our children to eat less."

A woman explains how her eleven-year-old son goes off to work for a month at a time—hard labor. Hard labor is $8 a month. Another boy has been away collecting wood for cooking.

"We don't know if our sons are alive or dead."

"We feel like we are in jail."

"We are grateful for your visit."

"We feel like our sisters and mothers have just visited us."

"We thank you for visiting us and we will pray for you."

I had about 3,000 rupees on me. There are 60 to every dollar. I asked the UNHCR staff if it would be okay to give these women the rupees.

"Yes, as long as we explain it is not from UNHCR, or they will expect cash will always be available in the future. Agreed?"

"Yes."

They were so grateful. These people are living day to day.

They give me some beads. They want me to come back.

But I can't help but wonder, if I do come back—maybe in a year—will they still be alive?

4:30 P.M.—UNHCR Field Office

We had lunch. We were all very hungry. I don't know what I ate but I was glad to have it.

Surkhab Refugee Camp

Three armed officers in uniform are traveling with us. Two are following us, and one is standing on the bed on the back of our truck.

I don't want to ask why they are necessary, but I assume that this might be a dangerous area for the refugees too. The camps are close to the border of Afghanistan and are at a higher risk.

At the camp I met a group of women who had been living here for twenty years.

"We came during the first war."

"We get old here."

They laid out mats for us to sit on and have tea. Their little daughters came out and sat beside them.

The women seem to enjoy making their embroidery. All the different pieces are beautiful. It takes them three months to work on each one. In America each piece would probably sell for hundreds of dollars. Here—if they're lucky and can get to a market to trade—they would get very little, the equivalent of a few dollars.

The women in this camp are not taught any other vocational skills, but they are asking and hoping for their children's future. One woman told me, "I am the third wife of my husband." In my ignorance, I did not realize that in this part of the world men can have many wives.

They show us a little stream of water in the camp. They are grateful they can drink from it when supplies run out. I am told the stream is not a healthy water source, but the drought has them drinking from it because of lack of supplies.

School is over. Boys come running out toward us.

They see we are taking pictures and want to be in them.

The boys were proud they knew some English. They all kept saying, "Thank you" and "You're welcome" and smiled a lot.

They laughed when one of us accidentally stepped in the stream.

We drive out as the sun is setting. The sky was clear and the sun was bright orange. The sun seemed so much bigger here than during any sunset I have ever seen. I notice a sign on the little mud schoolhouse. On a very big painted board it reads (translated):

UNITY

DISCIPLINE

FAITH

Friday, August 24

Here everyone prays five times a day

I have also seen many graveyards. There are branches with fabrics attached to them blowing lightly in the wind. There are a few tall white stones. I see women gathered near a grave in the corner. I think of loss. I think of my family.

I notice several goat herders. They carry sticks. One boy is about ten years old. He is with about twelve goats. They have shaggy black hair. I notice a few people sleeping under blankets. Between 12 and 2 many sleep to avoid the hottest part of the day.

Loralai Refugee Settlement

This morning we visit the Loralai. Inside we stop at the school run by Save The Children.

Painted on the walls is—

WELCOME

KNOWLEDGE IS POWER

WE WANT PEACE ALL

OVER THE WORLD

There is also a map of Afghanistan painted colorfully on the wall. We visit with the girls first. They sit cross-legged on the floor. The room is dusty. They don't care. They are happy to be in school.

Their teacher asks them, "How many of you were born in this camp?"

They all raise their hands.

"We want to be in our homeland. This is not our place."

They are learning Pashto (their native language).

In sixth grade only about one-fourth of the class are girls. The village puts pressure on them to get engaged. Only the sons work. One girl smiles at me and warms my heart. Another girl reads. Others sing a song. The song is translated for me. It is about the reconstruction of Afghanistan—about unity for the different tribes. Here is part of the song—translated: "In this critical moment how is our friend our enemy? You have come to visit us. You are our friend. We want to bring greenness and happiness to our country."

These young people need to have strength to rebuild. They need to be a force. The people running the school said, "We are glad you came to see us. We work hard and the children work hard. We would like to continue our program."

They worry about the closing of the programs from lack of funding. A sweet little barefooted girl makes her way to the front of the room. She has a dusty scarf on her head, white with little brown flowers on it. She holds up an old, thin notebook.

She begins to read a poem.

"We promise to work to learn.
Learning is exciting.
We don't want fighting.
We want peace."

One of the UNHCR women we are with starts crying. An elderly man also cries. He has to turn toward the wall. Then I start crying. The woman said, "We want Afghanistan not divided in pieces. Please, please—peace."

Young boys line up outside. They are wearing dusty plastic sandals. A little one walks in and goes up to the chalkboard to show us he can write. He writes his words in the direction of right to left.

I ask him what he wants to be when he grows up.

"Mula." ("Like a priest," someone says.)

Other children smile and say they want to be—

"Teacher."

"Doctor."

"A lawyer for justice" (an eight-year-old boy).

"In the government."

They are also all sitting cross-legged on mats on the dusty ground. They stood up, one at a time, as they answered. They are all smiling—so happy to be asked what they want to be when they grow up.

I ask, "Where do you want to be to do all these things?"

"Afghanistan."

The teacher came up to me and handed me a piece of embroidery. She said, "One of the girls in grade five wants you to have it." She said, "To thank our visitor." I went to say thank you. They were practicing reading and were very proud to show me.

These girls want to know my name. They know nothing of my life. To them, I am someone who came here to observe and to help. They are so sweet to me.

The man running the school said, "Please do not forget us. I feel we are close—no distance between us." We are all close. I could never forget them.

We stop to visit "the vulnerables." They are new arrivals but UNHCR must say "vulnerable." Three hundred families have been relocated here from Quetta. Now they will be living in an even poorer area. They will not be settled enough to send their kids to school. There is very little left here at this camp to give them. All stocks of items have been emptied. It is very hard on the staff when they do not have enough to give to all the refugees. WFP is already giving as much as it can.

UNHCR is providing water from a water tanker and giving all the supplies they have.

An elderly woman begins to walk with us. She shakes my hand very lightly—very gently. People here are not used to shaking hands. It is a new custom for them, but they make a thoughtful effort.

Several men are busy trying to build some small mud houses. The women have no help getting wood for fuel, and there is not a tree in sight for miles.

"How can we cook for our families? We have so little wheat flour, but we cannot even cook the little we have if there is no wood for fire. First we look to God and then to you people. We ask for help."

These refugees originally came from Meymaneh. It is one of the most northern cities in Afghanistan. They came a very long way to get here.

I asked, "How did you travel?"

"Through deserts and mountains. Most of the journey we walk. A short part of the journey we travel on donkeys." The trip took them over six weeks.

I asked a child, "When you lived in the city [Quetta], what did the children do during the day?"

"Every day we would try to work in the market, but so many times we could not find work."

A woman explained, "We faced a lot of harassment in Quetta. The police here in the camp do not harass us—so we are more peaceful. We ask only for a little food and assistance."

As we drive out of the camp we see the water truck coming in.

All the people are so happy to see the water truck—especially the children. They look like it's Christmas.

This moment certainly puts life in perspective. We stop the truck and get out to watch them distribute the water.

Most people cannot pay 100 rupees per family per month for water—so they drink from the stream. They are getting sick with dysentery.

Malnourished children with diarrhea often die.

Without more financial assistance they are afraid they will not be able to run the water pump too much longer.

We are shown how the pump works. Young boys stand off to the side and stare with serious faces. They have been listening to us talk.

Suddenly the water starts. The boys run under the pump. We all smile and laugh.

As I got back in the car I realized how much I am going to miss these people.

I anticipated I would feel for their situation and care once I saw these faces. How could you not? But I did not know I would feel like if we had more time we would all be very close friends.

As we looked at each other there was a shared understanding between us.

We shared opinions, laughter, artwork, loving our husbands, and wanting a future for our children. Wanting to feel we have a purpose in this life.

Our last stop is at the Basic Health Units. There are two in this camp. Each one is helping 10,000 refugees. There are only two doctors for both units. There are only two doctors for 20,000 refugees—one male doctor and one female doctor.

The Basic Health Units are very well organized. They give monthly reports to UNHCR. The doctors here are very proud that the children have all been vaccinated.

The biggest health problems are dysentery in children, and during winter, respiratory infections.

The female doctor is speaking to a woman. When the woman sees us she quickly covers her face completely with her head scarf. Only one eye is exposed. We catch each other's gaze as the others are welcomed by the doctor. The woman grabs a burquah off the floor and puts it over her head. Suddenly she is completely covered (body, shape, and face) by a large blue tentlike garment. It was like a blue sheet with small holes— many very tiny small holes over her eyes.

I want to look at her through the holes, but I don't. I want to smile at her, but I don't know if it's appropriate. I do anyway. I can't see her face at all to see how she responds.

I am told today is TB (tuberculosis) day.

A woman and her brother are sitting outside waiting for results.

A small white refrigerator is storing the vaccinations.

"No electricity—it is running with a hose to a gas tank."

A little girl with cerebral palsy is lying on a white sheet as her mother and a helper try to give her physical therapy. She is calm and quiet as they move her arms and legs.

We drive back to Quetta. It takes us three hours.

Suzy stopped to take pictures.

I stepped outside. In the middle of nowhere—no shade, no shelter.

I think about those women and children who walked in this scorching heat for almost two months. I can't understand how they survived—carrying all their worldly possessions—and with hardly any food. And how did they find water?

I can't imagine what it must be like for some refugees when they arrive somewhere and are told, "You are not welcome in our borders or in our camps."

Pakistan already has an estimated two million refugees. Many estimate it to be even higher.

How good it must feel to find a group of people like these UNHCR field officers, who welcome you and want to help you—who take time to listen to your story, and to register you and your family so you can begin to apply for assistance.

Imagine being given food after nearly starving to death.

No wonder these refugees are grateful for so little.

During our three-hour drive back we sat in silence as we traveled across the dry land. There was no radio. It was a long time for me to think.

Urban Refugees in Quetta City

There are three different types of Afghan refugees here in Pakistan.

The first came here twenty years ago during the war with Russia.

The second came in 1995 and 1996 when the Taliban took over.

The third came because of the current fighting as well as the drought during the past three years.

Here in Quetta City even the refugee children work.

It is not that different from refugee camp life in the countryside. One difference is they can have access to a trade, but they have to pay rent and pay for education (unlike in the camps).

Here, children are often kept out of school to work hard labor days. The Drop-in Center is where, for one hour, street children can have an education. One hour is all the time they will take away from working. That is their focus. The center tries to give them incentives like bread and tea to get them to come in.

This center is funded by Oxfam and Save The Children. These children are taught numbers and basic literacy skills. They are also taught hygiene education—how to clean and take care of their bodies.

The doctors tell us, "The children need to learn because many of them go around collecting garbage for work."

"When they complete their basic learning, we provide tea and bread and a first-aid kit."

I met a little boy with big eyes and many cuts all over his dirty hands. He told me he works collecting rubbish, and he receives two rupees for one kilo of rubbish. Two rupees is the U.S. equivalent of two cents ($1 = 63.95 rupees and 1 rupee = $0.0156372).

He is smiling and seems so innocent. He has no idea how unfair this situation is.

I asked a few others if they also collect rubbish. Most of the children raise their hands. The other children work with the parents in the market.

I asked one child, "Do you want to go back to Afghanistan?"

"Yes, but it is never going to be free there."

"Who wants to recite the ABCs?"

They all raise their hands and try to be first.

One little boy is chosen. He stands with his hands very politely behind his back. In a very sweet high little voice he begins,

"ABCD. . . ."

I am crying. I can't do this. One more room to visit.

I am standing near the entrance. I am not permitted to enter yet. I see a pile of little shoes. I walk in. They all smile. They are all so kind to a stranger.

"*Asalaamu alaykum.*"

Their story is the same. I think this is the hardest thing to see, to listen to them with their bruises, dirty torn clothes, cut fingers, as they smile at you. They are children. They still dream. They seem so full of hope, it breaks your heart.

As we drive away from the camp, all the children run out, line up by a wall, and wave good-bye to us. While in the car, Zahida and I tried to discuss the programs and Convention on the Rights of the Child—but we were crying.

We kept seeing more little children in the street collecting garbage.

I have no words.

Saturday, August 25

We flew back to Islamabad. I feel like it was a month ago since we were here. I'm very tired.

I meet Bernadette at the UNHCR office here. She is taking us to the first place. Bernadette used to work in Phnom Penh, Cambodia, and she had a message for me from Marie-Noëlle (who I was with in Cambodia). We spoke of our friend and Cambodia.

(A few weeks after we said good-bye in Bangkok, Marie-Noëlle was suddenly given notice of relocation. A few weeks later she was working in the UNHCR office in Sri Lanka. I wonder how she's adjusting. Sudden relocation is common with UNHCR. It's one of the difficulties of their jobs.)

It is a comforting feeling to be connected to each other around the world.

To respect and appreciate other places and cultures together is very much the spirit of UNHCR and its staff. It is the essence of the meaning of the United Nations.

Aga Khan Health Services

Dr. Javeed Akhtar Khan is the program officer.

The staff is half professional and half volunteers. The volunteers work for "religious blessings."

Everyone here has a common goal. They assist and try to heal many Afghan refugees living in urban areas.

UNHCR hardly has enough funds to help the over one million in camps. They can't also help refugees in urban areas—anywhere from 700,000 to 2 million, impossible to count.

There is also a small group of non-Afghan refugees. The non-Afghan refugees in Pakistan number approximately 1,700, and they are from Somalia, Iraq, and Iran. They are based in the major cities and receive limited assistance from UNHCR. UNHCR provides them with subsistence allowances to meet basic needs for food, housing, health care, and education, as well as legal aid and counseling regarding their status and other issues. UNHCR also seeks to identify durable solutions for them. We enter a room with about twenty-five women.

"Our children cannot go to school." "Many of our husbands and brothers cannot get jobs." "It is very hard to pay rent and school fees."

How do they survive at all?

Some of their fathers sell fruit, and many mothers work in Pakistani houses.

"We don't know about our future." "There is no future for our children." "Ten people live in one room."

I ask, "Any police harassment?"

"Of course. Usually they are just trying to get some money from us."

I am told they are always being asked to show their ID or passport.

Even those with these documents still may have to pay. One man tells us a story of a friend who showed his passport to the police and the police tore it up in front of him. It was his only identification.

"It is our fault—we live here illegally. This is their country. So what can we do? We can't live in our country. We will die. So what do we do?"

I ask, "How do you explain the situation in Afghanistan?"

"Terrifying."

"What is your message for the world—for the international community, for the U.N.?"

Suddenly they all start to speak.

A woman translates.

"We want peace. We want to continue our education. If we can go back to Afghanistan one day, then we can help our people."

They have to charge women and children for their lessons. It is very hard for them to ask for money, but this is the only way they can run the schools.

"Even if they can only pay a little, that is okay. We will still teach them."

This woman is smiling at me, and she speaks to me in a kind, helpful voice, trying to help me understand.

"The neighbors in this area don't want us here. We are always in danger."

Another woman speaks up. "We have been here eight years. My children have had no education for eight years. They have no future."

"The U.N. should help us. Please, we need help. Otherwise it is impossible to live here."

How do you explain to these women that there are not enough funds? The outside world only wants to help so much.

A woman wants me to know that many people have come here to talk to them, but they do not receive enough help.

"But at least here in Pakistan we are alive. Although we have many difficulties, we are grateful to be alive."

We visit the children. I meet an eight-year-old boy. His two front teeth are missing when he smiles.

I ask him, "What do you want to be when you grow up?"

"A doctor."

"Do you work?"

"Yes, I make carpets."

He shows me a big cut on his finger.

The children all stand up in unison. In their little voices they said, "Good afternoon, miss," and when I left, "Good-bye, miss."

These refugees have to study in different shifts between 7 A.M. to 10 P.M. The adults study at night.

I was invited to a community theater where young children and teens performed a play about a boy who didn't want to go to school.

He walked around the stage with a walkman on and had a very bad attitude. After a while all the other kids convinced him how school can be cool. The play was both funny and serious and very well acted.

Later on they had a music concert playing traditional and modern Afghan music.

These artistic programs were specifically organized for the refugees.

All the young people acting and dancing and singing were between the ages of three and seventeen years old.

I realized not only how important these performances are for them, but also how they would not be able to have them in Afghanistan. All plays, movies, TV, dance, and music are forbidden—these are all banned by the Taliban.

I want to get a list of what the Koran actually teaches compared with the Taliban's interpretation of the Koran's religious laws and sacred teachings. I think that it is important for all of us to understand and know the difference.

Sunday, August 26

I am on a plane now flying to Geneva.

I am out—that is what it feels like.

There were moments when I felt I escaped hell.

Now I have been pulled out and lifted up.

I met so many good people surviving in horrible living conditions.

I can't seem to think straight.

It will take me a while to recover from this trip, and of course, I hope I never do.

The mind wants to forget because it hurts and weighs so much on the heart and soul.

I am tired of crying and feeling so helpless. I want to breathe again—just for a little while. Then I will do whatever I can to help these people. How could I not—once I met them, once I saw for myself.

Postscript

About two weeks after this journal was written it was September 11, 2001. A day so shocking and so tragic it is beyond words. The world, rightly so, came to the aid of the victims and family members in New York City.

Not forgetting the Afghan families I had met just weeks before, I spoke out about their need for relief and I personally made a donation. In the days that followed I received three death threats, including a phone call (how he got my number, I still don't know). The man told me he thought all Afghans should suffer for what they did in New York City and that he wished for everyone in my family to die. Emotions were running high, I understand that. It was a difficult time for everyone.

Two years later New York is rebuilding where the Twin Towers once stood. UNHCR has helped 1.9 million people return to Afghanistan. Still, it will take a long time and strong consistent aid from the international communities to rebuild the country.

Mission to Ecuador

On June 6, 2002, I undertook a mission to learn about and assist refugees under the care of the United Nations High Commissioner for Refugees (UNHCR) in Ecuador.

Colombia is by far the most serious humanitarian crisis in the Western hemisphere and has one of the worst internal displacement problems in the world. Official government statistics put the number of internally displaced persons (IDPs) since 1995 at 720,000, while nongovernmental organizations (NGOs) estimate the figure to be closer to 2 million. According to the national Association of Financial Institutions, 158,000 Colombians left the country last year. Thousands of them have applied for refugee status in other Latin American countries, North America, Europe, and elsewhere. Although its mandate worldwide is the protection of refugees, UNHCR has been working with IDPs in Colombia since 1999 at the invitation of the Colombian government.

Since the collapse of the peace process in February 2002, clashes between leftist guerrillas and right wing paramilitary groups have intensified, causing more displacement and bringing untold suffering to the civilian population. On May 2, in an incident that shocked the world, 119 people—including 48 children—died in the northwestern district of Bojaya, when a homemade mortar hit a church crowded with civilians fleeing the fighting. On May 26, 53 percent of Colombian voters elected Alvaro Uribe Velez as their new president. Mr. Uribe, who will take office in August, has promised to take strong action against the FARC (Revolutionary Armed Forces of

Colombia) and other irregular armed groups and bring the forty-year-old conflict to an end.

Thursday, June 6—7 A.M.

Sitting in the L.A. airport, realizing it's been eight months since I've done a field visit. I've visited for individual days here and there when I've been able, but there's something selfishly I've been missing. To be gone away from this material world and completely surrounded by the urgent, focused life. Everyone focused on their own or someone else's survival. Basic survival and struggle to protect family, country, freedom.

This will be my first night away from my son Maddox. First time I am away since we came together three months ago. It was ridiculous how emotional I felt kissing him good-bye. Leaving him with my mom and brother. Realizing that family is so important.

And those friends, the ones who feel like family.

Then there is that rare occasion when strangers become family, like these aid workers I am about to meet. Everyone I am about to meet. They're not family. They have made strangers their priority. You can understand why fast friends are made.

Ecuador is one of the smallest countries in South America. It is slightly smaller than Nevada, with a land area of 276,840 square kilometers (106,476 square miles). Only two countries border it: Peru to the south and the southeast, and Colombia to the north. Chimborazo is the highest point at 6,267 meters (20,560 feet). Ecuador's mountain Cotopaxi in the Andes is the highest active volcano in the world. Ecuador has a population of 13,184,000, of which 65 percent are Mestizo (Indian and Spanish), a quarter Indian, 7 percent are Spanish, and 3 percent are black. Ecuador has 22 provinces, and gained its independence from Spain in 1822.

Warm greeting off the plane by ACNUR (Alto Comisionado de las Naciones Unidas para los refugiados: UNHCR in Spanish). It was true what the UNHCR staff told me, "You will feel like you have family all around the world." Drawn to similar places, similar goals for the same people, for the same reasons. I believe if asked why, they would all say because refugees or displaced people are arguably the most vulnerable people in the world. And if you've met them, they are also some of the strongest, most beautiful, most capable people in the world. Amazing survivors.

The staff here mentioned how it is difficult to get the world's attention here. The fighting, the war in Colombia, going on for forty years now, seems only to be getting worse. The violence is on the news but not the victims. Not the people. Not the families.

There are no large camps. Everyone is spread out in shelters, etc.

I am also told it is hard to get refugees to be outspoken, allow media access, because they are in fear of combatants who also crossed over the border and want them to remain silent. I am told, "It's not paranoia—many have been killed."

Since we arrived at night, I am brought straight to my room in the guest house. I find extra blankets and a little heater. I'm glad it's colder than I had expected. I think they knew it would be. The ladies here had bought a poncho for me in case I didn't have enough warm clothes.

Friday, June 7—7:15 A.M.

Breakfast, where we will start the briefing.

The first UNHCR office in South America was established in Buenos Aires, Argentina, to assist victims of the institutional breaches in the region. In the '70s, UNHCR opened a regional office in Lima, Peru. During the '90s, the new regional office was set up in Caracas, Venezuela, to cover northern South America and Panama for the victims of the internal conflict in Colombia. The situation became increasingly worse, leading to the opening of UNHCR offices in Bogotá and three other provinces in Colombia. In 2000, another UNHCR office was created in Quito, Ecuador.

I am told that every day people are displaced in Colombia. Then someone says, "And every day people are killed." I am told I will see a difference from the other countries I have visited. The refugees here are mostly urban. They are in small numbers. They are mostly professional people. They are not farmers. They are people who are used to living similarly to you, I would guess, the people reading this.

The U.N. is working together to have a "common house." U.N. specialized agencies are encouraged to have common premises wherever possible in the field. In Quito, UNHCR and other U.N. agencies have their offices in the same building. It would seem like an obvious thing for everyone to work hand in hand, but it is not always the case. I am told the Secretary General has been pushing the unity more and more. Here—WFP, UNDP, UNICEF, and UNHCR—all U.N. agencies work together.

Most democratic countries are not supposed to. It should be very unusual. Colombia is democratic, but agencies like UNHCR, Red Cross, etc., have to help protect the people.

Protection is a word repeated often in the conversations this morning. The protection of an estimated 20 million uprooted people is the core mandate of UNHCR. The agency does this in several ways. Using the 1951 Geneva Refugee Convention as its major tool, UNHCR ensures the basic human rights of uprooted people and that refugees will not be returned involuntarily to a country where they face persecution. Longer term, UNHCR helps civilians repatriate to their homeland, integrate in countries of asylum, or resettle in third countries. Using a worldwide field network, UNHCR also seeks to provide at least a minimum of shelter, food, water, and medical care in the immediate aftermath of any refugee exodus.

After the briefing, I am overwhelmed by the complexity of the situation. I'm in a bit of a haze, but one thing I can already tell—there is much I feel I should have known. One would think with the humanitarian crisis as extreme as it obviously is in this part of the world, the human rights violations would have more media coverage. So I—we—all would know about it.

Seventy-four percent of the territory of Colombia is controlled by guerrilla or paramilitary groups. (The majority of the 40 million people live in the 25 percent of the main cities still controlled by a democratic state.) That is mostly border areas where they control resources—drugs, oil, coffee, emeralds. So who is buying from these people? Who buys these exports? Who is supporting the rebels?

In this 74 percent of the country, the government is absent or very weak. There is no national protection in those areas. The Catholic Church is one of UNHCR's main partners here. That is true for all of South America.

My visit this time is only in Ecuador. I am reminded I am only seeing a small part of a very big operation. Venezuela and Ecuador bordering Colombia and Colombia itself have UNHCR offices. UNHCR is also covering Panama, but the border is a swamp jungle, one of the most inaccessible parts of the world. UNHCR is also covering Peru, but the border is jungle, same as the Colombia-Brazil border.

More briefings: massacres and kidnapping—3,000 per year. An average of nine or ten people a day.

Even though in the last three years more and more people are fleeing Colombia, the majority of people—civilian victims of conflict—remain in the country. A high amount of IDPs. It seems harder to get aid and awareness. Maybe harder for the international community to understand the severity of the situation. Recent figures now show between 500 and 900 people are displaced every day. I ask why do they stay. A UNHCR staff member told me that one reason is they have a better chance of getting a job inside Colombia.

The long-standing armed conflict in Colombia has left hundreds of thousands dead and displaced more than 1.5 million people. Thousands have fled to neighboring Venezuela, Panama, and Ecuador. In 2001, some 2,000 asylum applications by Colombians were registered in Ecuador, compared with only 30 in 2000. During the first half of 2002, there were 2,198 asylum applications. Also, Colombian refugees ranked seventh in the number of asylum applications submitted in the industrialized world between January and May 2002.

Four years ago the presidential campaign was won by talk for peace. Last February the peace process failed. This election was won by talk of war. To use force to deal with the situation—I can only imagine how this new way will affect the people. Humanitarian aid workers are preparing today for the conflict to get worse.

I visit an office inside a church to meet asylum seekers or those who have already been given refugee status—to hear their stories. Erta Lemos is the Office Director for the Committee for Refugees, one of the UNHCR's partners here in Quito. She says she is very happy to be the missionary for migrants. She has a nice smile and wears a crucifix made into a ring on her wedding finger. On the walls are all the UNHCR posters of children around the world. One looks just like Maddox.

Erta explains to us how this office works. It opens at 7 A.M.

to accept people who are seeking asylum. Worst cases are people persecuted by paramilitaries. Most cases are single parents or children alone. Many cases are people who have been tortured.

"These cases also need emotional and spiritual support," she says.

First is a brief interview to see if they have a case for seeking asylum. If so, they start to fill out forms to document their case. Then a series of interviews. The office receives about twenty-five to thirty cases a day. Each case size is different. Some are one mother plus seven children, so that case is eight people. The office works closely with the Ecuadorian government on behalf of the people seeking asylum.

As we meet, I see people through the window begin their interview. Like other interviews where I have seen the person seeking protection, they seem broken, almost defeated. Their body language is the same—head slightly bowed, holding on tightly to any papers or packet they have.

As we enter, we walk through a hallway full of people. One man is walking his crying baby back and forth. A few children also sit along the wall. I can't tell but they seem alone.

I am told I am about to meet a man whose wife and children were killed in front of him. "Very traumatized but getting better." Erta just went out to get him. I'm nervous.

He is a little man, wearing a gray-and-black sweater and work shirt. You can see he has tried to dress well. With what little he has. There are so many holes in the sweater. His gray hair is combed back and his eyes are sad. I would guess he's in his late fifties. Kind face. Handsome man. Very gracious.

He explains he is from the same area where there was just another massacre three weeks ago. He keeps being reminded to please speak slowly so they can translate.

He had a small farm with corn. I think he's speaking fast because he is so uncomfortable with this memory. He seems to want to get through it as quickly as possible. "I even had a jeep," he says. Guerrillas started extorting money out of him.

He seems to get nervous. I wonder if it's because I'm writing. I ask them to tell him that I promise I will not use his name. That we just want people to understand the situation in his country.

He continues. The paramilitaries came to the village and started fighting the guerrillas. Guerrillas accused him of supporting the paramilitaries. There was a massacre. Seventy people in the village were killed. "We're not sure," he says. It was guerrillas. He's a little shaken when he talks and keeps rubbing his hands together.

He is asked a question in Spanish. Suddenly tears well up in his eyes and he can't speak. William says, "I asked him how his family was killed." I look at the man and he's looking at me as if he is saying, "Please don't make me talk about it."

I've stopped writing for the last few minutes. He was trying not to cry. William told him it was okay. He can talk only about what he wants. The man apologizes. Can you imagine? Someone apologizing because they can't tell you how their family was killed.

He stands up, lifts his shirt, and shows us two bullet holes. Nickel-size round scars now. "The sisters helped arrange medical attention. That was three years ago."

"UNHCR helped me start a small cafeteria-type business. I am better. When I came, I had only the clothes I was wearing."

He says the illegal armed forces are somewhere here in Ecuador. He has received death threats here.

"We didn't kill you in Colombia. We will kill you here."

I ask him why they consider people like him a threat. Because he was kind of a local authority in his old village and guerrillas were killed there. He takes out an old dirty wallet and unfolds a paper he obviously holds close. It is an official document. It is proof he has made a complaint and is worried about his security. Also another letter requesting resettlement in another country, because he does not feel safe in Ecuador.

As he left, we thanked him for talking to us. He thanked us for listening. As he was leaving, he smiled. William apologized for making him remember sad things. He picked up our empty coffee cups. I suppose out of habit. He cleared the office desk as if it was a restaurant table.

A few moments later, he came back in and handed me a small plate of food. William said, "He had cooked to share with our visitor." He smiled. I didn't know what to say.

A woman comes in next, carrying candles and flower arrangements to show what she does to make a living. She takes out pictures of her son. In one he is three years old.

"When we arrive." Another is a school ID card. "Eight years today." Her husband was a lawyer. A very prominent family. Her cousin was a presidential candidate. "He was killed." Her husband was working on a case.

"He received death threats that he should not defend that person." We ask why.

"Drug traffickers were the ones threatening, so the case was something to do with stopping them. My husband did not respond to the threats and kept defending. They then killed his brother. The government gave our family bodyguards. It became known that the drug traffickers were giving money to the bodyguards to kill them. That's when we finally fled. When we arrived, my husband could not work. The law is different and we are not from here. I had to feed my family, so I remembered I knew how to do this."

She points to the candles and flower arrangements she brought in. "The sisters here at the refugee center helped me start production to be able to make a living."

She continues. "Then my husband got sick and died."

As she continues to speak, she starts crying. She can't seem to stop. She is speaking very quickly now. I ask William what she's saying. She is talking about trying to make enough money to get his medicine.

He died and she is now alone with her son. She continues talking, but she is looking up out the window with tears streaming down her face.

"My husband died on the 16th of September."

We try to talk to her about other things—to take her mind

away from her painful memories. We talk about her flowers. I buy a few from her, to decorate the UNHCR guest house.

Next we meet a boy who just arrived from Colombia. Once again, he introduces himself, but once again, I'm leaving out his name for his protection. He's going to be sixteen on June 14. Twisting the top of his backpack. Big brown eyes— very open.

"I have two brothers—one is seventeen, one is fifteen. We are here now living with our aunt who is from Ecuador. No father. In January 2000, my mother was forced to join the guerrillas. They took her away and we went to live with our grandmother. The guerrillas allowed us to visit our mother every three months—March and June 2000. They were forcing her to teach them about computers and writing. Last time we went to visit, the commander tried to make me stay and join combat. My mother talked them out of taking me that day, but told me to tell my grandmother to move. My grandmother sold everything we owned to move. Three months later we heard our mother had escaped and was on the run from guerrillas, but also from the police because they now saw her as a guerrilla."

I notice one of his hands is dark red—a birthmark? Maybe a burn.

"Last April my grandmother died. We came into Ecuador illegally. We had to—we had no passports. We were very scared. I can't go to school yet."

I ask him when he gets older what does he want to be. Does he like sports?

"Yes, but I am a good student, when I can go to school. I want to be educated. But first I have to help my brothers, then I will help myself."

The next lady enters the room already very emotional. She apologizes. She was just talking to the sisters about why she left Colombia. She is twisting a ring on her hand. She had to leave Colombia because the paramilitaries killed her husband. She has nine children—five boys, four girls.

"They dragged my husband from the house a few blocks away and killed him. We were told we had two hours to leave. We went to the bus stop where a man noticed all of us crying. He felt bad and gave us some money so we could take a bus near the border. Me and my children ran across the border. A man in a truck stopped and asked us our story. I told him and he put us in the back of the truck under a blanket. I sold jewelry I was wearing so we could pay for a motel and some food. A few days later, the hotel owner gave us sweets to sell at bus terminals to make some money. I met another Colombian who told me of this place. To seek asylum."

She then came here. That was last December.

"I am legal now, so I can have a job as a cleaner. I pay rent on a small apartment me and my children live in."

She pulls out a paper—it is a certification that her claim for refugee status has been accepted. "Finally my children will be able to go to school permanently."

She is very happy the people here are very kind, very warm. "I am grateful to the people of Ecuador."

●   ●   ●

Two of the people we just spoke with mentioned how sad they were at the death of a nun who helped them. As we get back in the car, I am told the story. The nun they were referring to died in a car accident. Three other nuns were with her—two of them also died. The accident was from the brakes failing. This organization of Brazilian nuns has been working here over twenty years. The sister I just met with received a threatening letter saying that the brakes were fixed to crash and kill her fellow sisters, and that should be a warning to her. The message— stop helping Colombians.

We talk over lunch.

Most all refugees are wonderful people, but they are human. And there are millions of them. So of course there are some so damaged they are unable to come through this kind of horrible situation with clear minds. UNHCR staff have been attacked by refugees.

One story was of a man who was applying again after being turned down for asylum. (Reasons would be, for example, a criminal record.) He suddenly pulled out a can of petrol, poured it on himself and the UNHCR worker, and set them both on fire. Luckily the worker was wearing a leather coat and was able to pull himself out of the hold of the other man who was trying to kill them both. Both men survived with severe burns. Later, the UNHCR worker actually got a letter from the man who tried to kill him, apologizing and explaining how desperate he was and asking for help. But remember, as they say—for every one like that, there are a thousand who remain patient and kind. Who live peacefully without anger.

The conversation turns to the woman we met who makes the flowers and who spoke of her husband's death and how difficult it was to get money for his medicine—I am told during lunch later from someone who knows her case that the truth is, her husband realized what a burden he was and committed suicide.

We stop at a market—the Otavalos exhibit (goods and handicrafts)—a very famous market in this part of the world. I buy a hand-carved chess set—the Spanish against the Indians—and a little Alpaca sweater for Maddox. Amazing, beautiful, intense strong faces. Soft dark brown, leathered from the sun. All hands show signs of a life of hard work. Many men in fedoras with long black ponytails. Women in sweeping cotton dresses, embroidered with flowers. These people are such successful merchants; it is known they apparently trade with New York.

Small guitars, the base made from the shell of an armadillo.

They play what they say is tennis in the street, but they have no rackets—they use their hands and hit a very small ball back and forth. As I watch, nearby a man is playing guitar for his three kids. A simple yet very rich history and culture. Only simple because of their honest, straightforward way of living. To just be among them and walk in their streets feels better than home. There is something wonderful and different—I wish the world appreciated it. As we are leaving, someone says, "Here in Imbabura the main dish is guinea pig. You marinate the meat the night before, then they bake them with peanut sauce. Better than rabbit, low in fat."

I'm still not sure what I think of that.

We received another call about Lionello's luggage—it's in Milan and arriving at 11 P.M. He will have to drive back to Quito, two hours away. Moments later, another call—it's not coming after all.

Saturday, June 8

Up at 7 A.M. It's cold. Italy played football last night. Two in our group are Italian UNHCR staff. Trying to figure out the football score proves to be a little funny in the middle of nowhere. First they were told they won 2–0, then they lost 2–1. We're still not sure.

A few of us were still sleeping at breakfast and had to be woken up. Part of it, I am told, is the high altitude. Also that is the reason for itching. I was wondering why I was itching. Strange.

I miss Maddox. I can't imagine how the UNHCR staff does it when they are posted in a no-family duty station. They go months without seeing their children. You ask them about it and they will tell you how hard it is. Everyone has pictures, but then they say the people they work with—refugees—many have lost their children. So they at least know their families are safe.

We are now off to visit the UNHCR field office in Ibarra. It is small and shared with the local church. I meet with more UNHCR staff, along with refugees and asylum seekers.

We are now close to the Colombian border. We can't be on the border or closer, as it is too dangerous. This is the place after crossing the borders refugees would come for their first meeting. The office started in October out of necessity, because of the rising number of groups of people running out of Colombia. This office covers a 250-kilometer part of the border and is in constant contact with the field office in Colombia.

Many young people who don't want to participate in war are crossing over. One of the main reasons for income-generating projects (skills training). To give them an alternative in life.

I meet another sister from Brazil, also with a crucifix on her ring finger. In 1998, the bishop of Ibarra was concerned with the forced migration Ibarra was receiving. The bishop asked the missionary sisters to help. The numbers now are even higher than in 1998.

In this office, like most all UNHCR offices, there are social workers, lawyers, protection officers, volunteers, registration and program officers, from all around the world. They have set up a safe house that I will be visiting later.

Between January and June 2002, there were 3,000 asylum seekers and other people of concern (vulnerables) and 1,000 refugees in Ecuador.

The UNHCR staff is noticing a rising number of minors fleeing forced recruitment. They tell me now I will talk with their friends from Colombia. A couple—a family with a small child (four years, I guess) and a boy who seems on his own. The man carries a guitar. I promise again not to use their names in the journal. They nod in approval, say "yes, important." Even though they are here, they still have concerns for their safety. They (the couple) show me on the map where they are from in Colombia. When leaving Colombia, the roads are most difficult. Every ten kilometers, checkpoints are set up by paramilitaries, with the next ten-kilometer checkpoint set up by guerrillas. The paramilitaries have lists—death lists—and they take documents. Sometimes they burn cars or just kill people. Sometimes a family of eight starts out and only three arrive. Because of this, many people arrive very traumatized.

"We left our home on the 10th of October last year. The guerrillas threatened my husband."

They say something in Spanish—everyone smiles. They are Protestant. They were having a vigil that night. They went away from their home for a night. They came home and their house had been burned. UNHCR has pictures.

"We have three sons and one daughter. What belongings didn't burn we gave to our children."

They are smiling at me as they tell this story. The little boy is sitting on the lap of a staff member, eating banana chips.

"What next after they burn your house—so we now had to leave."

They arrived in Ibarra on the 22nd of October.

"We love our country," she says, "but we love our life even more."

Next is the man with the guitar and his wife. He was in charge of a small farm. "It didn't belong to me, but I was in charge."

Armed groups moved in. Paramilitary and guerrillas. You're never sure who is who because they have no uniforms.

"Sometimes they would stop and say, 'Give us things—food.' I would always say yes, without asking who they were. On October 25, three men came by—close to the house this time—and asked for food. I didn't know some from the other group was spying/watching. I was on my way to the shops and was stopped by two men. At 7 P.M. it was a bit dark, but I could see behind them—there were more men."

They said, "You are a helper of guerrillas. I knew then they were paramilitary."

"Empty your pockets," they said.

"I did. I put everything on the ground."

"Pick up your ID card." They took it.

"Now we can trace you all over Colombia. We can kill you." (It is common for paramilitary to take ID cards. They have computers and networking across the country.)

"They told me I had twenty-four hours to leave or they would burn my house with my family inside while they were sleeping. So I left with my wife and child Fernando."

When he says his name, the child looks up and smiles. He has a cough.

"Luckily we knew some people in Ecuador so we stayed there for eight days."

You didn't want to stay near the border? I ask. Everyone laughs. The boy says he is too scared to talk. An irregular armed group was trying to recruit the boy, and he had a very hard time when they tried to recruit him. The man wants to play a song on his guitar. Since the elections, there are more forced recruitments. I don't know or understand UNHCR's position on this situation, but I think it would seem clear to anybody—the different groups are trying to build up their armies in preparation for war.

They all walk us to the cars as we leave. The families shake my hand and say thank you. I feel bad—I've done nothing for them.

Next stop—carpentry workshop, vocational training. UNHCR loaned money to Jose if he agreed to take time to teach and employ other refugees.

The father of the president-elect of Colombia was killed in a kidnapping attempt by FARC. So he has reason to hate. Some people are worried there will be even more fighting. Violence causes only one thing—more violence.

Many people here are called Jose. They joke that Jose in South America is like Mohammad in Arab countries. I meet a man named Jose. He had a furniture shop when he was in Colombia.

This place started in February. In March they began work. Jose is very proud—they have completed five sets. They have trouble distributing—no place to showcase.

"They can take advantage because we are refugees and more desperate to sell."

They have a warehouse out. So they don't consider it a bad lifestyle. "We want to encourage proper skills, jobs."

They are already trying to contact big shops in cities. Colombians are very enterprising people.

We walk over to some young boys hovering in the corner. One boy—he's new—is too shy to talk. Two twins—I hand them a Polaroid camera to play with. They take each other proudly, holding the football we brought. Jose shows us a place in back they are growing beetroots, carrots, and lettuce. He talks about ways to give more people jobs.

"I know it is hard for new arrivals to find a job, and even when you become a refugee, it is still hard. We don't want people to have to go around begging."

I ask how he came to be here. To be a refugee.

"Luckily—or unluckily—I was given a contract to make furniture for the army. Then the guerrillas got mad."

Then—as usual—he was threatened. He had twenty-four hours to get out.

"I took a suitcase. I lost everything. I put my family on a plane. Luckily I had enough money to do that."

At night he rode his motorbike.

"I was stopped by a man with a flashlight. I saw they were wearing boots like guerrillas do. I thought they were guerrillas. I was shaking. I gave them my documents when they asked. I don't question. I lied and said I had a doctor's appointment very early in the morning, so I ride at night. They did a check. I realized then they were the army. I was not on their list."

The army warned him there was a nearby guerrilla checkpoint and to be careful. He was scared but kept going and made it.

"Thank God."

I ask him if he would like to go back to Colombia.

"I think every Colombian would like to go back to Colombia. But we must have peace. My kids are going to school here and that makes me happy."

One little boy says that maybe he will join UNHCR when he is older.

"You are doing well," William says.

Jose answers. "When you have good will and you work hard, you get by."

As we leave, I notice the new boy—the quiet one—leaning in the workshop doorway. I wave good-bye. He gives me a little gesture of a wave and goes inside. Now we leave for what they call "the safe house."

For safety reasons, there are no U.N. signs, flags, or any markings on the outside of the house. People stay ten to fifteen days on the average—never more than a month. As the door opens, a little girl of maybe two in a little white dress comes to the door. This place is for vulnerables, single women with many kids. All people living here work together. Everyone has chores so they can take care of themselves. They run this place themselves. There is a room with nine sets of bunk beds. (Men and women have separate rooms.) I don't go in. One man looks very sick and is in bed. In the women's room, a little girl is asleep on a bed: "She is from a family who just got here last Thursday," someone says.

I then meet a little girl who was living for a while in the UNHCR office. She looks like a little angel. She is a special case, because she is a rape victim.

Suddenly, a man starts having convulsions. He passes out on the floor. The other men go to him. One holds his head, the other shakes his arms. He has had mild epilepsy all his life, but it's become much worse from trauma. He is twenty-seven. They carry him to bed: "He will be okay." To watch them come to his aid and know they were all strangers two weeks ago— now it looks like a family. Helping each other out in the most difficult situations.

They have a little, very basic kitchen. A young boy of about eight is helping his mom in the kitchen. He has a bold personality and holds out his hand. "*Buenos dias.*"

UNHCR has helped me organize and purchase school notebooks and supplies for the house. We bring them out and put them on a table. It is amazing to see children so excited about educational materials. There are also books for the adults. The mother quickly grabs one by Gabriel García Márquez and smiles. We also bring a few toys, and when we say it is okay to play, the kids upstairs come bounding down. It's great.

One of the women has been here eight days. She worked with an NGO in Colombia (to reform guerrillas) called Reinsercion. She tells us her story. She worked to help former guerrillas to reintegrate back to civilian life. To learn to live a normal life again. She took them to farms funded by the government to learn to work in a new way. (As she talks, a little girl is learning how to jump rope nearby. Other kids sit against the wall reading new books.) Because she worked with former guerrillas, the paramilitary are after her. They have taken over the farm. She was left with nothing.

"No time to even pack a suitcase," she says. She would like to join an NGO in Ecuador.

"I believe I have a lot to offer. I am an agriculture special-ist. I have many plans to help the people help themselves."

The woman also spent time trying to convert or convince people to convert coca plantations to other types of farms with different crops.

"It is very hard because they make so much money with coca, even very poor peasants. How can you tell them to work for crops that make less money? You can see the people of Colombia or any country where there is poverty and corrup-tion—there must be possibilities for survival."

She starts crying. "When they took the farm, they killed three people who worked with me. We had a kindergarten for the children of the people who were working on the farm. They also killed the teacher."

She dries her eyes with a tissue, gathers herself, and says, "I know that I have to start again and God will help."

I look at pictures she brings out of the farm. All the things they had accomplished to make things better. So much hope and promise in the pictures. Good people trying to help their country—help each other. She knew a woman who worked with human rights and was told about UNHCR. So she came to Ecuador looking for them.

"Ecuador has its own problems. Their own people need many things, so I am concerned for the children. This is not their country. Their families have nothing. We need to help Ecuador, to contribute to their country so they can be able to help us here."

She motions to my notebook. Is it okay? I ask. "Yes," she says. She's glad I'm taking notes.

She adds, when she tells people she is Colombian, "They look at you like you are monsters. We are not all bad people. We are many good people."

William asks her if she would like to go back to Colombia. She looks at him like he is crazy. I'm beginning to realize these people seem to have a very fun sense about them; as desperate as they are, they seem full of life and have a passion to live.

"It is a beautiful country and I love my people, but I cannot go back. I know at least for a few years. The violence has to stop. We won't survive if we go back now."

The shy boy from the carpentry workshop just came in the door. He must have walked here. It seems a very long way. He is holding the soccer ball we gave him. He shows it and hands it to his brothers. He's now smiling and seems very relaxed. I meet his mom—she's lovely.

We meet a family—a single woman living with her six children in a garage. She had to leave because two of her children were being recruited by the guerrillas. South America is not like other countries where masses of people move together and live in a camp. Moving out of your home to someone else's country and community. Individual families. They show me all the things they are making. The young man says he was very good at *capoeira* (a Brazilian fighting style), and then rebel groups asked him to teach them. He agreed to teach, but then they wanted him to fight so he left the group.

"I refused to carry a gun or work to produce coca. They threatened me, but it is against my principles. After that we knew that if we stayed there, we would be killed. We left town toward the border. When we arrived, an aunt told us we were on a blacklist. We lost everything—sold what we could. We came here and started working with whatever we could. We had a restaurant but immigration closed it down because we didn't have our papers yet. Luckily they did not deport us. We learned about UNHCR. Now we have our papers in order."

Now they make handicrafts. They show us gift boxes, dolls, flower arrangements—and sell out of the garage.

"I would like to start a proper business. I could make good pizza."

The nuns invite us over to their apartment to freshen up. They are missionaries, so they live as plainclothes women. Suddenly I feel such a strange feeling. Maybe because I was raised Catholic, but when they show me their bedrooms I feel I shouldn't look. I'm not sure why it was so interesting to me that they had a small exercise-walking machine. I suppose we don't think of nuns exercising or being that human. One room has pillows on the floor and small wooden statues. She puts her hands together in a gesture of "this is where we pray." One of the sisters tells me of her years in Colombia. She says she has been a missionary for eighteen years, eight outside of Brazil. Her group of sisters was organized to help migrants. She says now she dresses in normal clothes. Then she takes off her crucifix ring to show me. She hands it to me to look at. I feel I shouldn't touch it.

"We are from Brazil. Our order works in twenty-one countries. We work with migrants. I love going to different parts of the world, different philosophies. And always, you learn a lot from children."

I tell them my mother is Catholic and will be very happy I spent time with nuns. They giggle. This is an experience that continues to prove there is bad and there is also good in every organization, every country, every religious group.

One sister says, "My dream is to work on the border of Mexico and the U.S." I tell her she is probably the only person alive with that dream. She smiles. We say good-bye.

"Maybe we will see each other on the Mexican border one day. You never know," she says.

Oh, one last thing they say—it is translated—they are glad Brazil won the last football match.

2:45 P.M.

We visit a refugee community in a secluded area. There are forty people—seventeen are children. It takes us a while to drive up to where they live. I am told they only have one car between them. They shuttle down to the bus. They arrived from Colombia two years ago from St. Augustine. Referred to as "an ancient place in Colombia." Their reason for leaving: "They took many of our children to take up arms. The guerrillas were taking over. We are a spiritual community."

Up here in this secluded area they have a school and church.

"We have peace finally."

They are in the middle of nowhere; still they want to make sure no pictures are taken.

"We are afraid they will come get us."

We are taken to the kitchen—it's a woodshed, very organized. There are wooden benches and tables under a plastic sheeting. They are very welcoming and made a lunch of beef, rice, and soup. They tell me about the man they follow—contemporary philosopher Samael Aun Weor—whose teachings are about how humans can get better. A culture of human beings in search of God. The essence of the book of this philosopher they follow is that all religions are essentially the same. Maybe reincarnations of each other. From Buddha to Jesus. Following of a few thousand in Latin America—not a sinister cult.

"We have no political or economic aims. We teach our beliefs for free—open to anyone. No distinction of race, ethnicity, or social origin."

Some people here are not refugees. One family is Ecuadorian. They were given help to build a school, but still need windows and school supplies.

I don't speak Spanish, so all of these conversations are always being translated. I'm beginning to feel like someone who is a deaf mute—I don't want anyone to try to speak to me because I feel so bad I can't answer. I ask what their needs are.

"Water. Electricity. Draining for sewage. We do have one generator but it's not enough."

We ask a Colombian man about his life. Before this place, his life was in his country.

"There I sold tools and lumber—I was a tradesman. But rebels extort money from all businesses and no security in towns makes it impossible to have a shop. The land here is not good enough for crops."

He motions to me. "You ask a lot of questions. Must be very interested."

When it is explained that I was keeping a journal for people to read, he said, "You are a messenger between those who have nothing and those who have very much. That is a nice thing."

We played a little with the kids. I now realize all you need to break the ice with kids (especially little boys) all around the world is to bring a soccer ball. We brought gifts and they saved the wrapping paper for the school. We (UNHCR staff) started talking about that as we left. We exchange stories of amazing things we have seen refugees make out of plastic bags, wire, etc. Everyone agrees one of the favorites are the cars they make out of wire, to push and race. Also when they twist up pieces of plastic bags to make ropelike parts, then weave them together to make baskets. They tell stories of families who touched them or crazy things like a couple carrying a pig over the border and on a boat ride to safety; the pig—apparently scared of the boat—had to be put in a pillowcase-type bag. Surrounded by people who are so excited by the people they have met over the years. They think refugees are amazing, and they talk about them as friends.

We were early on our way back so we stopped to see the pyramids. Got out—met with a man with old red baseball cap, jeans, worker boots, traditional sweater, chewing a piece of grass. He leads us up a grassy hill.

"This is one of fourteen pyramids."

It takes me a while to realize I am in a valley of strange-shaped hills, all with ramps, and that we are actually standing on one. If you clear away grass and dirt, you uncover buildings made of clay. Symbols on top for them to tell time.

A local guide told us that the Quito and Cara merged and became known as the Quitocara. Two cultures that lived before the Incas. Settled here around A.D. 500. From here they resisted the Incas for twenty-five years. Under previous leadership, a matriarchal culture. A few items of ceramics have been uncovered.

Volcanic flint rock was used to reflect light and to communicate. Other ways to communicate—smoke, light, and sound. You have to wonder how much we have evolved. Or maybe the question is—how much better is our quality of life than theirs was. The question more so for the people of this region involved in today's war.

On the way back to the car we pass a corn plantation. A family with many kids—the older ones here to help their parents work, the younger ones play. Work is finished today and they are waiting for a bus. It's late. The father borrows William's phone to call for help. The kids are eating the corn stalks like people eat sugar cane. I take a bite out of one. It's sweet.

We talk at dinner about the difficulty of aid in the region. UNHCR, for example—its core mandate is to help refugees.

But over the years UNHCR has, out of the world's necessity, also begun to help IDPs (internally displaced people). But UNHCR is dependent for 98 percent of its funding on voluntary contributions from governments and other donors. They have hardly enough to take care of the core mandate. Last year from budget cuts, there were many jobs cut.

Someone at the table explained the problem of IDPs for UNHCR perfectly: It is as if you are a parent of four children. You are just getting by. You hardly have enough to feed them and you find two abandoned children you know you should adopt. If you don't, you know no one will. So what do you do? Somehow you have to find a way. If no one else in the international community is focusing on helping the over 1 million IDPs in Colombia—these are human beings—then you have to find a way. What is at stake is individual lives, families. We also spoke of other places and peoples of the world. Something I have found to be a very regular thing for UNHCR staff when they sit down together. It's wonderful. I wish the world could spy on these dinners and hear what I am hearing—they talk of the IDPs in Angola, the situation in the Congo, the Kurds and how they have been forgotten, Abidjan and why it is important to understand the situation there. We also talk of Panama—another part of the situation in this region. Another country affected by the Colombian conflict. We start to make plans for a visit in July.

Sunday, June 9

Breakfast at 7 A.M. Ecuador lost last night 2–1. Lionello comes down—luggage? No, it wasn't there. At breakfast, talk shifts to Venezuela. I can't quite figure out exactly the situation. People are taking their money out of the banks.

The Venezuelan president Hugo Chavez is a controversial figure and his country is deeply divided over his style of leadership and some of his policy decisions. His opponents have been calling for his resignation through street marches and strikes. His followers have also been marching in support of his government. On April 11, the Venezuelan army removed Chavez from power after a number of protesters were shot dead during a march. A nonelected provisional government took power in Venezuela but most countries in the region condemned the move as unconstitutional. Next day, Chavez's supporters in the army and in the poor neighborhoods of Caracas rallied around him and demanded his return. Chavez was released from detention and restored to power. Venezuelan society continues to be deeply divided and the continued political instability has negatively affected the economy.

Also in Colombia there has been a demilitarized zone during peace talks. Full of guerrillas, bombed today by army. Over forty killed.

Airport

We drive up to chain-link fences. One of the UNHCR staff—
Grace—went ahead to open the lock with a military official.
Bag check. Person check. Then inside, where we meet more
UNHCR staff. We are flying for thirty minutes, when suddenly
out the window, there is thick jungle as far as the eye can see.
The Amazon. Breathtaking. As we descend we begin to see little houses, then a small town. We are now in Lago Agrio—
"sour lake"—also called Nueva Loja. We are going very close
to the Colombian border. This part of the border was famous
for FARC crossing through and over. Apparently even armed
forces need rest and I am sure they also have other reasons. But
apparently there are fewer crossing because the paramilitary
has taken control of much of the land on the Colombian side
of this border.

We meet with more UNHCR staff—Ann and Rene. A
misty rain fills the air. Someone says it's been raining for two
months. This area is rich in oil—natural resources. But the
wealth is unfairly distributed. Very poor people don't see
the money. Here there is 70 percent poverty, 21 percent extreme poverty. Until the month of May there was no electricity. Probably the most violent part of Ecuador. Recently there
were 68 executions. Over 80 percent of the people killed
were Colombians. Half the refugees coming to this place are
children.

Rene works inside Colombia in Putumayo. High percent-
age of illegal armed groups in the area. Many people are perse-

cuted by guerrilla or paramilitary groups or caught in between fighting. In that area of Colombia, government presence is weak. In Putumayo alone there are 10,624 IDPs—60 percent between infancy and seventeen years old. In Narino, there are 16,218 IDPs. Those are official figures of registered persons as of the end of May. Everyone believes there are many more who are just not registered. In all of Colombia it is estimated there are almost 2 million internally displaced people. The number of IDPs has grown after the collapse of the peace process. There has also been an increase in single female heads of households, most probably from forced recruitment.

The roads between Putumayo and Narino are very bad and it is difficult for staff to move around. Health care is mentioned. It is the state's responsibility (as a democratic country, etc.) but they are unable to care for those trapped in the land controlled by the illegally armed groups. (Again—that is 74 percent of the land.) Norwegian People's Aid, an NGO, finances part of the church's activities.

Rene also says now that after the peace process collapsed things got worse. Years ago you could walk the streets at night—now with all the killings it's too dangerous.

The briefing has been going on for a while now. I'm having trouble focusing. So much information. So many important things to understand. Maybe I'm feeling the altitude. Like most people, I prefer human contact to graphs and pages of reading material. Yet I know I am so lucky to get this information, to have briefings, because unfortunately, if you just watch the news, you can't understand fully the situations around the world.

Marte also speaks about how difficult it is to get people to talk only about thirty kilometers from the border. U.N. coordinator explains, as you can imagine, that protection for the staff—for all organizations—is the priority. For example, we are in contact with the ICRC (Red Cross). When one person goes out on a mission—just to be cautious—he alerts them: "If you don't hear from me after this many hours on this day . . ."

In the car to a shelter Ann is talking about a refugee girl of twenty with leukemia who died. The International Organization for Migration (IOM) helped to get medicine. (Not U.N. but very closely associated—they did a lot of work in the past with people coming out of Kuwait.) But for the girl it was too late. Ann says it was very sad—she was in a lot of pain the few days before she died. No one could get morphine or any type of good painkiller.

"It was very hard to see," she says.

We reach the shelter. Construction finished in 2001. The IOM is going to help with water, plumbing.

"We are still having problems," Ann said. Twenty-five persons live here now. There is a child-care center and place for women to work. They have room for 400 and tents in case of an emergency mass influx. There are gardens for women to work. We take a walk and meet about eight women working a garden. One man is also helping them. They are all from Colombia. They introduce themselves with a very gracious welcome. They say it is nice to have visitors. They are very grateful to all organizations for help.

"Please continue to help us. We will work hard."

We ask one woman to tell us her story.

"I have ten children—nine are with me. Paramilitaries gave us fifteen minutes to leave. After we arrived here, they took my son and whipped him. They took him—we haven't heard from him."

She gives us his full name. His nickname he would recognize, and she tells us he was a great football player.

"Please try to find him."

Another woman is not only willing but wants to speak. She first shows us how she does laundry—a wood paddle, a bucket, and a plastic cup.

"Both groups forcing our children to join them, so we ran to here. But now our problem is that my husband is sick—prostrate."

We visit a school-type room where the mothers have gathered with their children. So beautiful. Babies. One looks sick—keeps fighting. One little girl asks if we have a doll. "My father can't buy a doll."

We had brought gifts, including two dolls, but they have to share.

"But I wish I could sleep with one."

I meet with a twenty-year-old and with three children. We ask her what they need.

"Legalize our papers so we can work and don't have to go back to Colombia, where we will lose our children to war."

These are nice people, decent people. I meet a father.

"Sixteen years ago in Putumayo province I met my wife. We had a farm. We built a home, we had cattle. I was proud because I had something to give to my children after I die. I was not worried about my children. The way they expelled us was very violent. My wife and children were taken away. I was taken into custody. They humiliated us. They tortured us. I was not allowed to take anything, not even, the saddest of all, my wife and children. I gathered courage to ask what is going to happen to my children and my wife. In so many words—they were killed. They told me, 'We did what we had to do—don't think about them anymore.' I was going crazy. After seven months I found them. I couldn't believe it. They were alive. That was the greatest happiness in my life. My wife was crying so much—she couldn't believe I was alive. They had told her, 'Don't worry about your husband—we are going to bury him properly.' We were reunited here in Ecuador. A friend we had in common recognized we were both here. Be at ten tomorrow at the park, he said to both of us separately. It was there in the park that we met. I couldn't believe it. My life was saved."

Another woman comes to talk with us. She is with an older lady—they are friends and help each other here. She is holding the boy I have been thinking is sick.

"I had to leave because the guerrillas took my son of sixteen—I never saw him again. I took my other children out of the country as fast as I could. I came by canoe in the San Miguel River. I told the driver I had no money but told him my story. He helped me."

I ask another woman carrying a small baby, "Why did you leave Colombia?"

"Because they killed my husband. I was scared for my life and my children's life also. One day my husband said, 'I'm going out to look for work.' He left at 7 A.M. At 4 P.M. they called his parents—could they identify the body. His body had been found just lying on the road. I hid at a friend's house and they said I should go to Ecuador. They had some money to help me make the trip. We—my baby and two other children—took a bus to the border. We had remembered to take our ID cards from the house—thank God—before they burned it. So we entered legally as visitors."

When did this all happen? I ask.

"Two weeks ago."

We're running late now so we have agreed to skip lunch. In the car on the way to meet a family, I talk with Rene from the UNHCR Colombia office. I'm now remembering how hard it is to write in a moving car.

We stop at a small two-story house—five brothers and their mother who arrived one month ago. A group of about ten children lean over the upstairs balcony to say hello. I am told it is $100 per month rent—they don't have the whole house. They didn't have water at first and had to clean up outside of the building to make it livable. At one point the owners threatened them that there were too many people. But later the owners were okay because "we are good and take care of the place."

Since they have been here, there have been a few incidents: They were stopped by police and accused of collaborating with armed groups "because we are Colombians." The police say there are problems in towns with refugees.

"We can prove they are professional people. The police

understood we are not criminals and let us go. We are still scared. We are close to the border and have seen both armed groups near here."

All stories are different but have similarities—threats by armed groups. One man worked for twenty years as a registrar with the government. The last two years he started to receive threats. Both armed groups want records and certificates.

"They force you to help one, then accuse you of helping the other," he says.

I'm given a drink. I've been so warned about the water, but I decide I'd rather get sick than be impolite. Rene also drinks.

We sit down with one of the fathers. He crossed with three children over three days and two nights. Were the children scared?

"Yes. We had to pass many checkpoints—three guerrilla, three paramilitary. The last one took our papers. It was hard to cross then legally. We suddenly had no papers so we were now illegal. We still have three sisters in Colombia. One was working as a nurse—we just received word she was just taken by guerrillas. We tell people we are refugees protected by UNHCR. That helps—helps to protect our children."

Another man says, "We have to leave because of the constant conflict—guerrillas and paramilitary."

He breaks down crying, then finally, "I had to leave my family behind—three children. They are being threatened."

Guerrillas have threatened to blow up the house where the children are. He is looking for help to bring them here to Ecuador.

"I want to tell you all you don't see in military kill-ings: Buses are stopped, people are taken out and killed. The children are traumatized by bombing, being a victim of cross-fire."

He starts talking, then stops and cries.

"I was tied up and they were going to kill me. I don't want to remember that. The two children I brought with me because they wanted to recruit them. I'm a doctor and I refuse to work with guerrillas. They threatened me. I have more to say but it's so humiliating—I want to stop."

We thank him. William and he hold each other for a mo-ment. Both men are fathers and can understand each other's pain.

We talk to Ann about how UNHCR can help his family in Colombia—the children who had to be left behind. What if they can make it to the office in Colombia, then can we help them from there? Yes, maybe—but they have to find a way to get there. Although many people feared an intensification of the war, President-elect Uribe has been talking about a new peace initiative. It is not yet clear what will happen in the next months in Colombia. The fighting that has been going on for forty years will get worse before it can get better. A final fight—war, maybe? Who will support them? How long will it take? What happens to the people? The families caught in the mid-dle? The almost 2 million already displaced?

End note: Lionello, Toby, and I were planning a trip to Panama to follow up on the Colombian situation from another border.

But as I prepare this journal for release, I received word that the situation has already become worse, making it too dangerous to go.

One final note: Lionello's luggage finally arrived the last day.

Afterword

The beginning of the United Nations charter is "We the peoples." It's one of the most beautiful things I have ever read—and that's what it is; this life spent together, all the people of the world, protecting our history, our cultures, and learning from each other.

Refugees are families and individuals just like us but they don't have the freedom we have. Their human rights have been violated.

The United Nations High Commissioner for Refugees cares for more than 20 million people. An estimated 8 million are children. Under the age of eighteen.

"Those who deny freedom to others deserve it not for themselves."

—ABRAHAM LINCOLN

Sierra Leone

As of June 2003

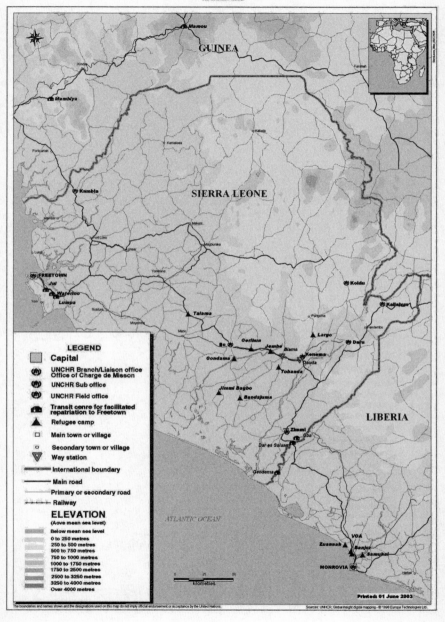

LEGEND

- **Capital**
- UNCHR Branch/Liaison office
  Office of Charge de Misson
- UNCHR Sub office
- UNCHR Field office
- Transit cenre for facilitated repatriation to Freetown
- Refugee camp
- □ Main town or village
- ○ Secondary town or village
- ▽ Way station
- International boundary
- Main road
- Primary or secondary road
- +++++ Railway

ELEVATION
(Aove mean sea level)

- Below mean sea level
- 0 to 250 metres
- 250 to 500 metres
- 500 to 750 metres
- 750 to 1000 metres
- 1000 to 1750 metres
- 1750 to 2500 metres
- 2500 to 3250 metres
- 3250 to 4000 metres
- Over 4000 metres

GUINEA

SIERRA LEONE

LIBERIA

ATLANTIC OCEAN

FREETOWN

MONROVIA

kilometres

Printed: 01 June 2003

Sources: UNHCR, Global Insight digital mapping - © 1998 Europa Technologies Ltd.

United Republic of Tanzania

As of June 2003

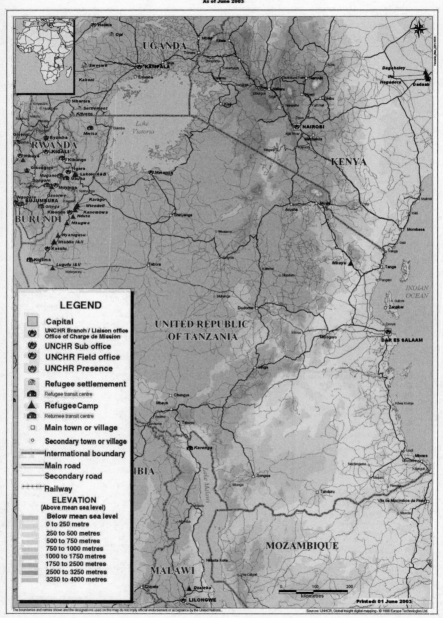

LEGEND

- Capital
- UNCHR Branch / Liaison office / Office of Charge de Mission
- UNCHR Sub office
- UNCHR Field office
- UNCHR Presence
- Refugee settlemement
- Refugee transit centre
- Refugee Camp
- Returnee transit centre
- Main town or village
- Secondary town or village
- International boundary
- Main road
- Secondary road
- Railway

ELEVATION
(Above mean sea level)

- Below mean sea level
- 0 to 250 metre
- 250 to 500 metres
- 500 to 750 metres
- 750 to 1000 metres
- 1000 to 1750 metres
- 1750 to 2500 metres
- 2500 to 3250 metres
- 3250 to 4000 metres

The boundaries and names shown and the designations used on this map do not imply official endorsement or acceptance by the United Nations.

Sources: UNHCR, Global Insight digital mapping - © 1998 Europe Technologies Ltd.

Printed: 01 June 2003

Cambodia

As of June 2003

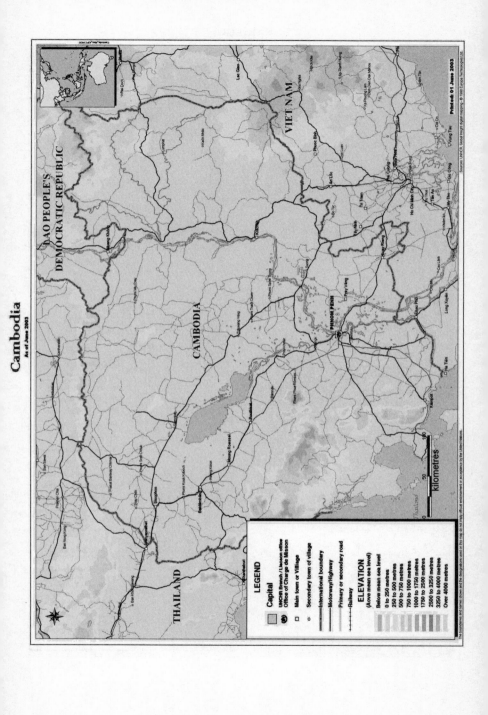

LAO PEOPLE'S DEMOCRATIC REPUBLIC

VIET NAM

CAMBODIA

THAILAND

PHNOM PENH

LEGEND

◉ Capital

⬤ UNHCR Branch / Liaison office
Office of Charge de Mission

□ Main town or Village

○ Secondary town of village

International boundary

Motorway/Highway

Primary or secondary road

Railway

ELEVATION
(Above mean sea level)

Below mean sea level
0 to 250 metres
250 to 500 metres
500 to 750 metres
750 to 1000 metres
1000 to 1750 metres
1750 to 2500 metres
2500 to 3250 metres
3250 to 4000 metres
Over 4000 metres

Kilometres
0   50   100

Printed 01 June 2003

Sources: UNHCR Global Insight digital mapping © 1998 Europa Technologies Ltd.

Pakistan

As of June 2003

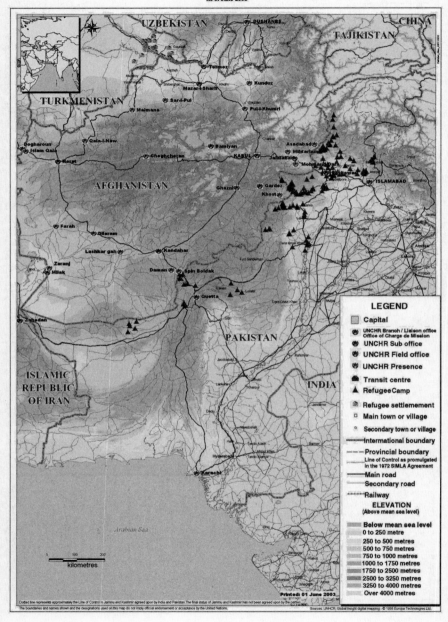

LEGEND

- Capital
- UNCHR Branch / Liaison office Office of Charge de Mission
- UNCHR Sub office
- UNCHR Field office
- UNCHR Presence
- Transit centre
- Refugee Camp
- Refugee settlement
- Main town or village
- Secondary town or village
- International boundary
- Provincial boundary
- Line of Control as promulgated in the 1972 SIMLA Agreement
- Main road
- Secondary road
- Railway

ELEVATION
(Above mean sea level)

- Below mean sea level
- 0 to 250 metre
- 250 to 500 metres
- 500 to 750 metres
- 750 to 1000 metres
- 1000 to 1750 metres
- 1750 to 2500 metres
- 2500 to 3250 metres
- 3250 to 4000 metres
- Over 4000 metres

Printed: 01 June 2003

Dotted line represents approximately the Line of Control in Jammu and Kashmir agreed upon by India and Pakistan. The final status of Jammu and Kashmir has not been agreed upon by the parties.

The boundaries and names shown and the designations used on this map do not imply official endorsement or acceptance by the United Nations.

Sources: UNHCR, Global Insight digital mapping - © 1998 Europa Technologies Ltd.

Ecuador

As of June 2003

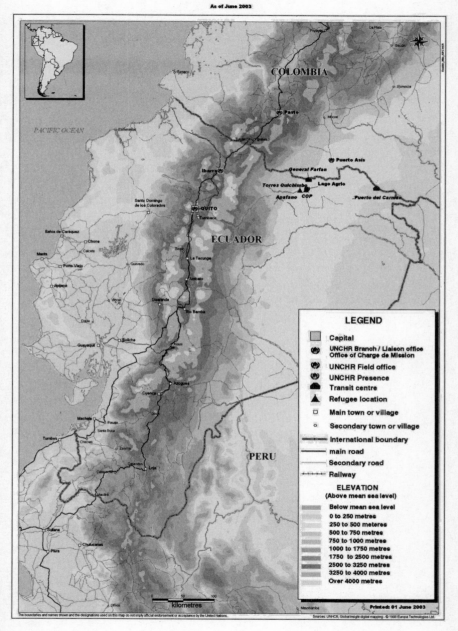

PACIFIC OCEAN

COLOMBIA

ECUADOR

PERU

Tumaco
La Plata
El Bacón
El Llorencia
Pasto
Mocoa
Esmeraldas
Zulumango / Ipiales
Puerto Asís
Ibarra
General Farfan
Torres Quichimba
Lago Agrio
Apafano   COP
Puerto del Carmen
Santo Domingo
de los Colorados
QUITO
Tumbaco
Bahía de Caráquez
Chone
Calceta
Manta
Porto Viejo
Sigsi
La Tacunga
Jipijapa
Ambato
Vinces
Guaranda
Daule
Río Bamba
Guayaquil
Boliche
Alausi
Azogues
Cuenca
Machala
Giro
Pasaje
Santa Rosa
Zaruma
Tumbes
Chacras
Loja
Catacocho
Cariamanga
Macará
Guana
Chulucanas
Piura
Mayobamba
Olmos

LEGEND

- ▢ Capital
- UNCHR Branch / Liaison office Office of Charge de Mission
- UNCHR Field office
- UNCHR Presence
- Transit centre
- ▲ Refugee location
- ▢ Main town or village
- ○ Secondary town or village
- International boundary
- main road
- Secondary road
- +++++ Railway

ELEVATION
(Above mean sea level)

Below mean sea level
0 to 250 metres
250 to 500 meteres
500 to 750 metres
750 to 1000 metres
1000 to 1750 metres
1750 to 2500 metres
2500 to 3250 metres
3250 to 4000 metres
Over 4000 metres

kilometres

Printed: 01 June 2003

Sources: UNHCR, Global Insight digital mapping - © 1998 Europa Technologies Ltd.